# HOW TO THINK LIKE A GNOSTIC

Jeremy Puma

How to Think Like a Gnostic

First Edition 2013

Published by Strange Animal Publications
**http://www.strangeanimal.net**

**ISBN-13:
978-0615823324 (Strange Animal Publications)**

**ISBN-10:
0615823327**

The author/publisher would like to acknowledge the generosity of the following contributors, without whom the publication of this text would not have been possible:

Richard Billingsley

Miguel Conner

Amy DeOrnellas

Coe Douglas

Spence Fothergill

Brett Hamil

Charles Hertenstein

Paul Hillman

David Morgan

Heather Nolting

Ronnie and Marilyn O'Daniell

Gareth Pashley

John Plummer

Andrew Smith

Matthew Smith

Kalyan VinnaKota

Thanks, also, to those who have chosen to remain Anonymous.

# TABLE OF CONTENTS

Dedicated to Spark

# Introduction: What is a Gnostic?

And, why would you want to think like one? Depends on who you ask. My conclusion is that a Gnostic is **someone who pursues gnosis within the context of a particular set of myths, most of which are represented in a number of Christian non-Biblical texts referred to as "Sethian."** [1]

In my humble opinion, there are a few characteristics found in the Gnostic texts that mirror some of the ideas found in Zen Buddhism, so when you put them together, they work really well. I call these the Four Truths:

---

[1] In my estimation, the finest current discussion on what it means to be Gnostic comes from the work of David Brakke. See especially, *The Gnostics: Myth, Ritual, and Diversity in Early Christianity*. Cambridge, Mass.: Harvard University Press, 2010. You can find a great interview with Brakke on Aeon Byte Gnostic Radio:
http://www.aeonbytegnosticradio.com/2012/07/true-identity-of-original-gnostics.html.

1. **Life is imperfection.**
2. **The origin of imperfection is separation from the Fullness of the Pleroma (the realms of Perfection).**
3. **It's possible to reconnect to the Pleroma.**
4. **Reconnection to the Pleroma is possible via this Way, the cultivation of gnosis.**

There's a story that goes along with this, similar to other religious stories. It has to do with the fall from grace of Sophia, or Wisdom, an aspect of Divinity, and her production of a being called the Demiurge, a misguided oaf of a deity who ended up creating our universe, but who didn't do a very good job. It's kind of a theory of "Unintelligent Design."

In the story, Jesus, as an aspect of the Mind of God, came to Earth to teach us this story, and each person's existence is a struggle between the salvific forces of Jesus, and the forces of the Archons, the rulers of Fate. Just how literally one wants to take this is up to each individual Gnostic. Some Gnostics are totally atheistic, and see the whole thing as a myth describing psychological processes (one of my friends doesn't believe that Jesus even existed, a position called "mythicism," with which I personally disagree). Some see the Archons as actual entities, like demons, but insane instead of strictly evil. We'll talk about these two different approaches a little later in this book.

You can find a bunch of different versions of this story in the Nag Hammadi Library (NHL)[2], a collection of extra-Biblical texts found in Egypt in 1945 (not to be confused with the Dead Sea Scrolls, which are from an entirely different tradition). The problem is that they're so fragmentary, and represent such a diverse range of thought, that it takes serious study to scratch the surface of them.

Most people who you ask, on the Web or in bookstores or neognostic organizations or popular religious websites, think that to be a Gnostic, you need to be into a weird kind of

---

[2] The best translation out there is the most recent, *The Nag Hammadi Scriptures: The International Edition*, Marvin Meyer ed., HarperOne 2007.

Apostolic Succession or the New Age Movement or hallucinogens or paganism or whatever. I don't find that this is the case, but those concepts are way more popular and lucrative than the idea that historical accuracy and actually trying to understand the Gnostic texts are pretty important if you're going to go around calling yourself a Gnostic.

In my experiences with the groups that promote these ideas, there's a lot of egoism, prevarication, and cultish activity involved; I think it's safer to approach the subject as a solitary practitioner.

Most modern scholars are starting to agree that there really wasn't an historical thing called "Gnosticism," which is why I try to avoid the term as much as possible. In my experience, you have to be really careful when you're looking into anything called "Gnosticism;" if something sounds like nonsense, or too good to be true, it probably is. It's important in this game to have a good BS detector.

Thing is, the Gnostic story is a difficult story. It's full of a lot of jargon and complexity, in large part because the story wends its way through tens of different literary formats and hundreds of spiritual traditions. There are a lot of different interpretations of this story out there, some good, some extraordinarily kooky. It's difficult to really "get" how to think about these myths and place them into a useful context through which you can navigate reality—a "worldview." This text, and the collection of essays and stories that follow, are intended to help the curious seeker do just that.

We'll start with an overview of the basic Gnostic myth, and look at how the themes and ideas found in this myth apply to the formation of one's outlook. We'll then present a number of essays from the perspective of the practicing Gnostic. I hope you find it worthwhile, and it at least makes you think!

# Part One: A Gnostic Worldview in Theory

# I. An Illustrated Gnostic Monomyth

The story that follows is an extrapolation of major themes from the Sethian creation accounts. This story is the foundation of the Gnostic worldview, and can be located, with variation, in a number of texts (*The Secret Book of John, On the Origin of the World, The Hypostasis of the Archons, etc.*).

Rather than try to sift through the differences between the texts, I've attempted to create an outline that contains all of what I consider their major elements. This run-down is pretty basic, but hits the points we'll be discussing in this book in a more concise fashion than you might find if you picked up a copy of the Nag Hammadi Library (NHL). Not to say you shouldn't, just that this might be a helpful guide.

So, let's begin at the beginning. Or, rather, before the beginning!

Before anything else was the **LIMITLESS LIGHT**....

We can't, in fact, even truly say that the Limitless Light

 **"WAS"**

because doing so limits it to a particular state of being, and it has no limit. It has no color, no shape, no size, nothing. There isn't even a good verb to use to describe it.

The only way to understand the LIMITLESS LIGHT is by BECOMING the Limitless Light, in its entirety, and since we are in the **WORLD OF FORMS**, we can't do that. The World of Forms, where we live, is limited by things like time and space.

Even "Light" isn't really an adequate term to use to describe the Limitless Light, because isn't like the light of, say, the Sun:

....or the light of a fire:

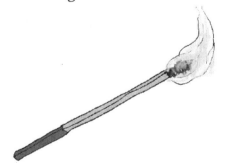

... or especially the light of a lightbulb:

It's simply an indescribable Light in which no darkness exists to contrast it. It's a lightless Light that can't be seen, a soundless Sound that can't be heard, an expressionless Passion that can't be felt.

It can't be measured, because nothing can stand outside of it to measure it.

Because nothing limits this Light, it contains

POSSIBILITIES

Of course, in a Limitless Light with no

# CONTRAST

the only possibility is binary: either it's the Limitless Light as Unity, one single Everything, or...

...isn't.

The only option of differentiation for something which has no limits is the experience of itself.

In other words, it can't rightly step outside of itself in order to experience itself, so it has to do so from within.

This necessitates a split within the Limitless Light. In order to know itself, for itself, the Limitless Light had to divide into Two. It did this with its first "thought," the Observed, the first differentiation within the Limitless Light.

We call THE OBSERVER "**GOD, the FATHER**," and we call THE OBSERVED "**BARBELO, the MOTHER**."

This has nothing to do with human gender—it's a rhetorical device we use to help us understand the roles of God the Father and Barbelo.

Since the two, the Double Source, still exist as parts of the Limitless Light, we consider them equals, both permeated by the Light. This permeation in which the Double Source emits is called the **PLEROMA**, or Filling Up.

In order for God the Father to observe Barbelo, Barbelo must return to the source, the Limitless Light, thereby giving birth to a third principle within her.

Her decision to return to the source was the third principle (the motion of BARBELO), that of the desire to return to the source that the Limitless Light might know itself. Thus, we say that Barbelo is the preexistent Virgin who gave birth to the all, the womb of the whole differentiated realm of BEING.

This principle is the Great Androgynous **CHRISTOS**, the perfected Son/Daughter of the Limitless Light as God the Father.

³

When God the Father gazed upon the beauty and wonder of the Christos, God gave him a share of Immortality and

---

³ Note the "vesica pisces," the familiar Christian fish symbol created by the intersection of God and Barbelo.

Imperishability and Perfection, which filled him with the Limitless Light, and supplied him with **NOUS**, the principle of Mind, through which the Christos could continue the process of differentiation that the Limitless Light might continue to know itself.

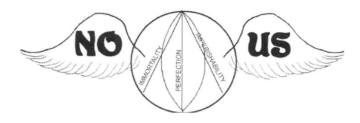

The Christos, with the Mind, desired to continue the process of differentiation by returning to the Source, the Limitless Light. In so doing, the process continued and the Limitless Light began bilocating further, splitting into all possible Doubles.

These Doubles are called the **AEONS**, as they exist in a time beyond Time, as projections of the Limitless Light in his manifestation as God the Father and Barbelo and the Christos.

The Doubles are not split into straightforward opposites, but instead are split into neutralizing Twins of differentiation. Imagine the process of Creation running backwards—the Twins come together in a flash of light and ascend into undifferentiated spirit-light.

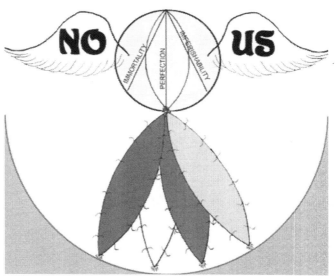

This whole process of emanation still takes place within the Limitless Light, which uses the process to learn about itself.

In the realm of all possibilities, one possibility will always be limitation. Since all possibilities must occur for the Limitless Light to truly know itself, inevitably a limit arises, beyond which one's wisdom becomes incomplete. Eventually, the process results in **PISTIS SOPHIA**, Faith Wisdom.

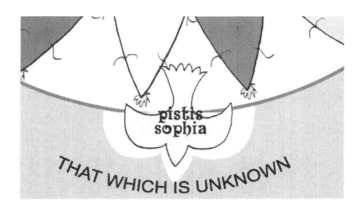

## This Aeon always lies farthest away from the source of the Limitless Light.

Desiring to know what lies beyond this point—in other words, to participate, through ignorance, in an act of creation—Pistis Sophia gives birth to **YALDABAOTH**, the **DEMIURGE**, also called Saklas or Samael, a serpent-shaped being with the head of a lion. Yaldabaoth is thrust into the realms beyond the perception of the Limitless Light, into the Void beyond the differentiation, the World of Forms—our realm of perception.

As with any newborn, Yaldabaoth's attention is drawn towards the sound and the light. Looking beyond the border between he and his mother, Yaldabaoth sees the Pleroma, obscured by the border of ignorance, and assumes that he perceives his own reflection.

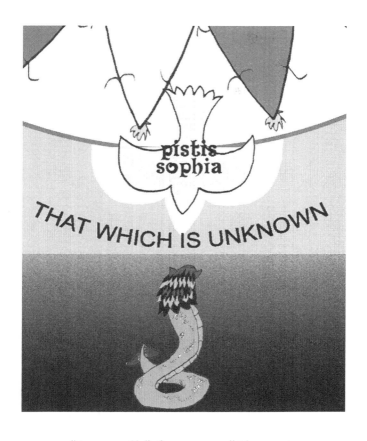

"I am all," he says. "There is none apart from me. I am the **ONE TRUE GOD**."

Sophia, peering down in repentant realization of her error and wishing to save her child from the darkness of ignorance, replies, "Child, you are in error! My child, come through to me!" (Which translates, so says one text, to YALTA BAOTH.)

This realization, that something greater than he exists, drove Yaldabaoth mad with envy and jealousy. This is why he tells us, in a Demiurgic Verse within Scripture, **"I the Lord thy God am a jealous God, visiting the iniquity of the fathers upon the children unto the third and fourth generation of them that hate me."**

# The true God, the Father, has no others of which to be jealous.[4]

Choosing to ignore his mother, the disobedient Demiurge cast her from his realm, but only after he had been tricked into stealing a portion of her Limitless Light:

This portion in hand, he set about creating his own material realm.

---

[4] See the *Secret Book of John:* "But by announcing this he indicated to the angels who attended him that there exists another God. For if there were no other one, of whom would he be jealous?"

Yaldabaoth separated the energy from the matter, the land from the water, the Earth from the Heavens.

He didn't truly separate them, but set up the illusion that these things are separate, indeed, that all things are separate from one another. This is because he was separated from the realms above by the abyss of ignorance, which kept the Limitless Light from knowing that part of itself.

After creating these distinctions, the Demiurge began mirroring the Aeons from above in the form of the **ARCHONS**.

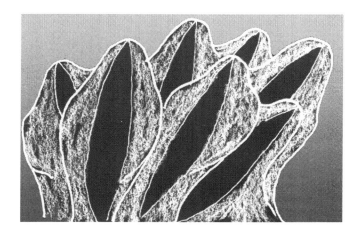

These Archons, numberless, are ruled by Seven Kings and Twelve Princes—the days of the week and signs of the Zodiac—and mirror the divine Twin Aeons of the Pleroma.

Yaldabaoth and the Archons then set about creating the Garden of Eden, and placed Sophia's portion of the Limitless Light into the Tree of Gnosis, JUST AS SOPHIA KNEW HE WOULD.

Finally, hazily recollecting the image of the Divine Androgynous Christos, Yaldabaoth and the Archons set about creating humankind. Thus do the Demiurgic Verses tell us, in the plural and not the singular form, that Yaldabaoth and the Archons created mankind as male and female to mirror the Aeonic Twins of the Pleroma. "LET *us* MAKE MAN IN *our* IMAGE, AFTER *our* LIKENESS.... SO GOD CREATED MAN IN HIS OWN IMAGE, IN THE IMAGE OF

GOD CREATED HE HIM; MALE AND FEMALE CREATED HE THEM."

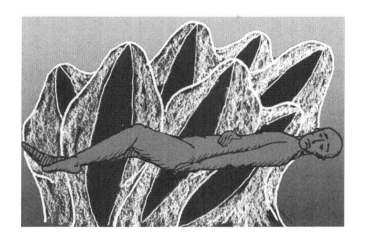

The Demiurge breathed life and a soul into the lifeless body he created, but the body would not stir, as it contained no portion of the Limitless Light.

Meanwhile, Sophia had returned to the Aeons of the Limitless Light and had repented of everything, and a plan had been set in motion. God the Father sent Aeons into the realms of the Demiurge, where they took the form of the Archons, saying to him, "Bring forth the Light you stole from your Mother and breathe a small portion of it into his face that he might move."

**ÆONS in disguise as ARCHONS**

Saklas did just this, and the man, Adam, arose with a portion of Spirit.

**Such was the nature of the Spirit within him that the Demiurge and the Archons became jealous of their own creation and determined to remove the portion of Spirit from his body. Little did they realize that they were doing so according to the plan of God the Father.**

The Archons set Adam over the Garden of Eden, instructing him that he might eat of any of the trees of the Garden, but not the Tree of Gnosis; otherwise, if he ate of it, he would die.

They said this, however, according to the will of God the Father, who knew that if they told him this in such a fashion he would be more likely to eat the fruit.

The Archons then cast Adam into the deep sleep of ignorance and attempt to remove the spirit from his body. In so doing, they create the female, Eve, the image of Sophia and of Barbelo above her.

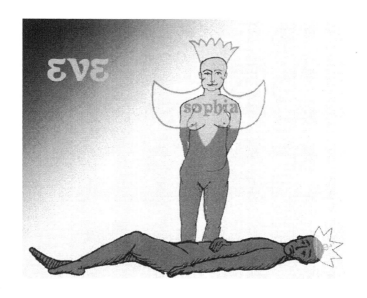

When Adam *awakens* and sees Eve, who contains a portion of the Limitless Light, the Spirit, she lifts her veil and he experiences the gnosis of Holy Sophia, and remembers his true nature as part of the Limitless Light trapped in the realm of Illusions. This is because they now both contain the spark of the Limitless Light, and recognizing this spark in others grants true wisdom.

Meanwhile, **Sophia**, **Wisdom**, appearing as a serpent,

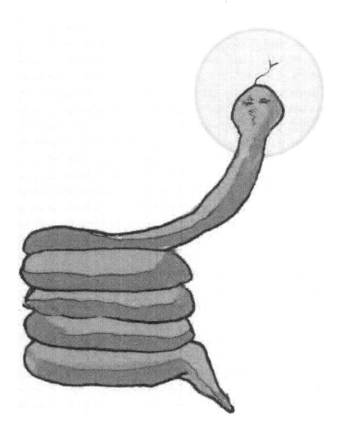

and the Christos, appearing as the **LOGOS**, or
the Word, in the shape of an Eagle,

descend into the Tree of Knowledge. **The Holy Sophia represents Barbelo, and the Logos represents the Christos, and this is why we honor both as our Saviours and comforters.** They instruct Adam and Eve to eat of the fruit, knowing that Yaldabaoth hid the Portion of the Limitless Light inside.

They did this knowing that by doing so the two would forever contain a portion of the Limitless Light and the Gnosis of who they're, where they came from, where they would go after they die, **AND THAT THEIR DESCENDENTS WOULD RECOGNIZE THESE THINGS WHEN AWAKENED TO THE SPARK WITHIN.**

**This is why we say, according to This Way, that GNOSIS = AWAKENING (WORD + WISDOM).**

Unfortunately, the World of Forms is too differentiated, too far from the realm of the Limitless Light's perfection to allow for redemption by the Totality. When the Archons see what happened, that Adam and Eve knew them for the false gods they are, they become incensed. Yaldabaoth sets off immediately after Adam and Eve, but they hide from him, ashamed to have been servants to a false deity, especially after their gnosis of the Limitless Light within.

Finding them, Saklas and the Archons decide to take a different approach to maintaining control over humanity and keeping them in ignorance. **They build a Prison of Black Iron, the World of Forms, and weave beautiful and appealing illusions within its walls.** The illusions stupefy Adam and Eve, who lose sight of their gnosis and perpetuate the race of humanity within the confines of the Black Iron Prison.

**THAT THEY CONTAIN SPARKS OF THE LIMITLESS LIGHT, HOWEVER, ALLOWS AN ENTRY POINT FOR THE CHRISTOS AND SOPHIA, AND HAS ALLOWED A SECRET UNDERGROUND OF AWAKENED INDIVIDUALS TO RETURN TO THE PRISON FROM THE REALMS OF THE TOTALITY AND ACTIVATE THE DIVINE SEED WITHIN EACH OF US, ALLOWING US TO ACHIEVE GNOSIS AND SAVING US FROM THE IMPERFECTIONS OF THE WORLD OF FORMS.**

Throughout history, again and again, the Christos and Sophia have returned to the World of Forms, allowing the Pleroma to expand within its walls. **No matter how many Empires the Archons manage to create, no matter how many times they strengthen the walls of the Black Iron Prison, they can't keep the Christos and Sophia from returning to us.** They tried to drown the entire world in a great deluge, but God the Father saved the family of Noah, who released Sophia's gnosis back into the world in the form of a dove. They established the archetypal Empire of Impelled Control in

Rome, but the Logos descended into Jesus Christ and awakened his disciples to the Limitless Light.

**They established the Empire of Total Destruction with the creation of the Atomic Bomb and its detonation in 1945, but the Logos and Sophia manifested months later in the collection of Words of Wisdom in codices discovered at Nag Hammadi.**

They continue to create Empire—as said Philip Dick, "THE EMPIRE NEVER ENDED"— but Sophia and the Logos continue to teach us how to resist, how to attain gnosis and thus bring about the redemption of the corrupted realms of the Demiurge.

# II. A Gnostic Worldview

So, why the big deal? What's the point behind this strange story, and why is it so interesting on so many levels, even though it's full of really, really odd imagery and seems to turn the creation myth from Genesis on its head? The deal is, **this story is an aspect of the Logos itself**– it's a manifestation of Divine Reason that is activated by its application in our lives. Done right, the application of the coded story causes the manifestation of Wisdom. It's a secret code with a hidden meaning that, once discerned, makes you go "oh, okay!"

I know, I know– I'm getting all flighty. Here's the deal, though: for me, and for some people, *this is a story that gives life meaning on an individual level*. From the Gnostic Monomyth, we can develop what we might call the **Gnostic Worldview**, an understanding based on the stories of what the hell is happening to us, and why it hurts when we stub our toe. It allows us to develop an understanding of what it means to interact with that which we perceive, and gives us a Way to measure whether or not our philosophy is any good.

**Question:** Do I have to have a worldview, or a philosophy?

**Answer:** I don't know, man! I'm not you! You probably already have one, even if you don't think you do. But that's totally up to you. I have one, and it helps me cope with stuff that's annoying or ridiculous, so I'm a proponent of finding a way of interacting with the world.

**Another Question:** Why should I care about this Gnostic Worldview stuff anyhow? I'm perfectly happy with my own religion/philosophy.

**Another Answer:** Great! Then you probably don't need to keep reading this, especially if you think it's bunk, or if you've already made up your mind about "Gnosticism" or something.

**Ooh, one more Question:** SCIENCE! Where is it? How do you "prove" this stuff?

**Answer:** TOTALLY something different here. For the record, I LOVE Science. Big fan of hard scientific discovery. I love modern medicine and think 85% of the "alternative healing" scene is crazy talk. I think hardcore creationism is silliness and has no place in schools except in discussions of literature or social anomalies. However: this book isn't doing Science.[5]

With this out of the way, let's take a look at the implications of the Monomyth. What does it teach us about the nature of reality and our place here? Keep in mind, once again, that this is my own analysis based on my own *gnosis*. You may agree or disagree, but my intent is that of those original Sethians who wrote the myths in the first place: I'm giving you a map based on my explorations, and you're encouraged to either discard the map and make your own way, or use the map to explore the features of your own existence.

Consider the discussion that follows a kind of Legend for the Map.

Let's begin with the most basic assumption, starting at the top, and work our way down, and see what happens.

---

[5] Before going any further, if you haven't yet, you should REALLY read an amazing post by John Michael Greer, on his site The Archdruid Report, about Science and Magic: **http://thearchdruidreport.blogspot.com/2011/09/clarkes -fallacy.html**. Although I wouldn't describe what this book contains as "Magic," his post really hits on the difference between what we're doing and Science.

# 1. The Limitless Light.

A big problem some individuals have with the idea of God is the question of whether God himself had a creator. If so, did God's creator have a creator? This results in an infinite regression, a pile of turtles extending down into infinity. As Gnostics, we solve this problem by stepping outside of the infinite regression and concluding that at a certain point, the regression has to stop. The Monomyth starts at this beginning (a good place to start!), at the most irreducible level, that of the Limitless Light.

The Limitless Light can't be described *in toto*, as to do so would limit it. Instead, we have to try to imagine it based on the idea of infinity. All points that ever existed, currently exist, and will exist in the future occur simultaneously within the Limitless Light. Since the Limitless Light is infinite, nothing exists outside of it. Think about it: infinity is everything, so it doesn't have any borders, because if you could step outside of a border, it would mean you weren't really in infinity!

As infinite dimensions, the Limitless Light transcends space and time to such an extent that what we perceive as motion, change and time would by necessity appear as a single unit to the Limitless Light, as it would perceive every instant simultaneously. Thus, we can define the Limitless Light as the absence of cause and effect. As soon as cause and effect arise, the Limitless Light becomes limited.

"Light" is typically used to refer to the knowledge of the presence of the Limitless Light, both internally and externally. When we refer to the Limitless Light above all things, we sometimes refer to a presence that fills all things like light fills a darkened room. The "light within" is the presence of God within, manifested through the medium of the Logos, Word and Sophia, Wisdom. Isn't solely the self or the soul, but a quality that self and soul can be said to possess when "enlightened," and an essential line of "communication" between the Self and the Other, the Subjective and Objective, the Limited and the Divine. When we act in a Christ-like manner, we're said to be expressing the Light Within just as the Christ refers to himself as "The Light."

Nonetheless, we don't place any kind of 'elitist' emphasis on the idea of the inner light. As Jesus says in the *Secret Book of James (NHL)*, "Don't be proud because of the light that illumines, but be to yourselves as I myself am to you. For your sakes I have placed myself under the curse, that you may be saved."

## 2. The Binary.

When discussing infinity, only two possibilities arise: completeness or differentiation. At this point, this is it: either nothing happens (completeness), or something happens (differentiation). Had the Limitless Light maintained its infinite nature, I wouldn't be writing this, nor would you be reading it. According to the Monomyth, however, the Limitless Light underwent the second possibility, and, in so doing, became conscious. In other words, the Limitless Light wanted to know itself. Since it was infinite, it had no way to do so from without (since nothing exists outside of infinity), and therefore had to do so from within.

This was the first binary, the division of the Limitless Light into two different aspects, one of which was an observer, which we call God the Father, and one of which was being observed, which we call Barbelo the Mother. With the creation of this either/or binary, the Limitless Light began the process of self-knowledge.

Now, since the Limitless Light is infinite and can't step outside of itself, the only way for it to know itself is by experiencing all of its possibilities, which means it began manifesting these possibilities through the medium of God the Father and Barbelo. Since these two aspects of the Limitless Light are, in reality, its initial "sense organs," we consider God the Father and Barbelo both aspects of the single, monotheistic Unknown God—the Limitless Light itself.

# 3. Barbelo.

*This is the first power which was before all of them, which came forth from his mind. She's the forethought of the All – her light shines like his light – the perfect power which is the image of the invisible, virginal Spirit who is perfect. The first power, the glory of Barbelo, the perfect glory in the aeons, the glory of the revelation, she glorified the virginal Spirit and it was she who praised him, because thanks to him she had come forth. This is the first thought, his image; she became the womb of everything, for it's she who is prior to them all, the Mother-Father, the first man, the holy Spirit, the thrice-male, the thrice-powerful, the thrice-named androgynous one, and the eternal aeon among the invisible ones, and the first to come forth.*

*The Secret Book of John, NHL*

————————————————

*Barbelo, for example, is the feminine principle providing matter for, and giving birth to, a perfect male offspring, the First-Begotten Son of the Pleroma (Self-Originate, Christ). She's also the "likeness" or "image" (eine) of God's immeasurable light responsible for the emanation of the divine Self-Originate, "a luminous spark." And finally, she's also Ennoia, the first vague conception of God's 'self ' which will, upon giving birth to Intellect (the Self-Originate), articulate her intuitive understanding of God into a coherent symbolic presentation and externalize the 'inexpressible' into a signifying chain of individual predicates.[6]*

————————————————

The Second Power, Mother of the Aeons, Womb of the Pleroma, Virginal Mother/Father, Daughter, Sister and Consort of the Invisible Spirit– Barbelo is all of these things, and more. Still, how is it possible to understand Barbelo, the First Emanation from the Invisible Spirit, the Matrix of the Ten Thousand Things? If you read the Sethian material, you'll find her described in all kinds of different ways. Is she a Goddess? Is she God? *What is the deal with Barbelo, anyhow?*

[6] Plese, Zlatko. *Poetics of the Gnostic Universe: Narrative and Cosmology in the* Apocryphon of John. Koninklijke Brill 2006. *p. 136.*

As humans, we can't help but anthropomorphize, and when attempting to discuss the feminine principle, we can't help but picture a woman. Sophia, for instance, often discussed as a higher manifestation of Mary (be she the Virgin or the Mother), is pictured in Mary's traditional garb and conflated with her more often than is likely warranted. The temptation exists to treat Barbelo the same way, to hold images of her as specific "Mother Gods" from various traditions. Doing so, however, doesn't result in any real insight about Barbelo. Applying specific images from foreign traditions or assigning human features to her profundity causes one to miss the True Gnosis of Barbelo.

Barbelo can be anthropomorphized but not pictured, because our relationship to Barbelo is the relationship of a beloved infant to its loving Mother while still in the womb. She's warmth, light, nourishment. She's a Presence who is One with the Father, for how is an infant in the womb able to differentiate between the Mother in which he rests and the Father's presence which he senses as well? She's comfort and peace and the first Restriction, as the Womb is the first limitation experienced by the ensouled child.

Sensual differentiation exists only as potential for the child in the womb, just as differentiation exists only as potential within the realm of Barbelo. The child in the womb can't describe the environment in which he grows in terms understandable to humanity, nor does he need to.

Barbelo gives birth to the Perfected Son, the "babe rushing forth from the womb" according to a famous poem attributed to quasi-gnostic Valentinus.[7] The infant, now manifested in the World of Forms, able to sense and differentiate sensations, begins to understand the Mother as Sophia, Wisdom, a quality unavailable to the ensouled while still within the womb of the Mother. This is how Sophia emanates from Barbelo, and does so through the medium of the Logos, the reasoning quality that awakens within the child and allows him to make the distinction between the World of Forms and the womb in which he has existed.

The infant feels love, can sense and experience aspects of the World of Forms that

---

[7] Valentinus, "Summer Harvest."
http://www.earlychristianwritings.com/text/valentinus-harvest.html

exists beyond the womb, but only through the medium of the Mother, of which he's still part. **She's the entire universe to him**, and the premanifested experience of the universe which she experiences and passes to her infant. The infant is the Image of the Mother and Father while still in the undifferentiated realm of the womb, and knows the Father through her but can't know God except through the inherited qualities of the Father and Mother which are present during this stage of development. This is the way the soul should come to know Barbelo, and meditation on this image can assist the earnest seeker in coming to know and love Barbelo.

Truly, any comparison or metaphor such as the one I'm attempting here can never really do justice to the Glory of Barbelo who exists before even the Pleroma. Nonetheless, if we can understand Barbelo as loving us in the way our mother loved us while we were gestating within her, we come closer to a proper understanding of the First Emanation. We can then honor her Properly as the Highest Female Principle who is also the Virginal Mother/Father, the source of divine nourishment and ultimately of the Highest Possible Love.

*Because of you salvation has come to us; from you comes salvation! You are wisdom! You are knowledge! You are truth! Because of you is Life; from you comes Life. Because of you is Intellect; from you comes Intellect. You are Intellect; you are a universe of truth.... Unify us according as you have been unified! Teach us the things you see! Empower us, that we might be saved to eternal life. For, as for us, we are a projection of you, as you are a projection of the one that primally preexists. Hear us first—we are eternal! Hear us—the perfect individuals! It's you who are the aeon of aeons, the all-perfect One who is unified.*

"Hymn to Barbelo," The Three Steles of Seth (John Turner trans.)

# 4. The Pleroma.

So, the Limitless Light undergoes the process of differentiation, introducing cause and effect into the mix. It does so in the only possible way—by extending itself through the process of iteration. "Iteration means the act of repeating a process usually with the aim of approaching a desired goal or target or result. Each repetition of the process is also called an "iteration," and the results of one iteration are used as the starting point for the next iteration."[8] The Limitless Light extends as God the Father and Barbelo. Barbelo returns to the source (iterates), the Limitless Light, because no other option yet exists. Nothing is beyond the realm of God the Father and Barbelo, so there's only one direction to go. After returning to the source, God the Father and Barbelo give birth to the Christos.

The Christos is the perfect androgynous reflection of the Limitless Light, and contains its mind, which we call Nous. If it helps, we might consider the Christos the

---

[8] http://en.wikipedia.org/wiki/Iteration

model of the conscious vehicle through which the Limitless Light explores itself. It does so by creating the Aeons, different qualities of the Limitless Light which expand to fill its infinite space. This "filling" is called the **Pleroma**, and it's the place in which the Aeons dwell, and also the process through which the Aeons expand and explore the Limitless Light.

## 5. The Aeons.

*For from the light, which is the Christ, and the indestructibility, through the gift of the Spirit the four lights (appeared) from the divine Autogenes. He expected that they might attend him. And the three (are) will, thought, and life. And the four powers (are) understanding, grace, perception, and prudence. And grace belongs to the light-aeon Armozel, which is the first angel. And there are three other aeons with this aeon: grace, truth, and form. And the second light (is) Oriel, who has been placed over the second aeon. And there are three other aeons with him: conception, perception, and memory. And the third light is Daveithai, who has been placed over the third aeon. And there are three other aeons with him: understanding, love, and idea. And the fourth aeon was placed over the fourth light Eleleth. And there are three other aeons with him: perfection, peace, and wisdom. These are the four lights which attend the divine Autogenes, (and) these*

*are the twelve aeons which attend the son of the mighty one, the Autogenes, the Christ, through the will and the gift of the invisible Spirit. And the twelve aeons belong to the son of the Autogenes. And all things were established by the will of the holy Spirit through the Autogenes.*
*- The Secret Book of John, NHL*

*Each one of the aeons is a name, <that is>, each of the properties and powers of the Father, since he exists in many names, which are intermingled and harmonious with one another. It's possible to speak of him because of the wealth of speech, just as the Father is a single name, because he's a unity, yet is innumerable in his properties and names.*
*The Tripartite Tractate, NHL*

---

We hear all kinds of stuff about the Archons, because they're such an interesting, immediate concept. They're the Ultimate Conspiracy Theory, a group of cloaked and tentacled figures who pull the strings of Fate, and who can only be defeated with knowledge. They're dark and mysterious and all goth-y, and humans sure do dig on the niftiness of the dark side of things.

Not many people in Gnostic circles, however, give a lot of space to the Aeons, those equally present– and arguably more useful and important– characters who dwell within the Pleroma, the higher realms of being available to the person who transcends the shadowy World of Forms. What the dickens are these Aeons, anyhow? They seem to have names, and are talked about sometimes as though they're places ("realms"), and sometimes as though they're actual beings. Are they like angels, or demigods? Or are they indeed locations, which can be inhabited?

The best way to explain the Aeons is through a little introductory Platonic metaphysics. "Good gravy, that sounds intimidating!" you may be thinking (or, you may be thinking, "Platonic metaphysics **again**?!") Either way, bear with me, because it's far less complicated than it seems, and there are some pretty cool ideas here.

To begin, let's look at one of the most complex, useful and fascinating objects ever devised by humankind:

What? Don't recognize it? You use it every day. In fact, you're likely using it right now. Maybe it'll be easier to recognize if I show you its more familiar form:

Yes, both of these things are, in fact, chairs. The top chair is the "Loopita Chaise Lounge Chair," designed by Victor Aleman, a

Mexican designer.[9] The bottom is, well, a standard chair.

This is a problem for Plato, who is truly interested in discovering what lies beneath the nature of reality. These two objects *seem* nothing like one another, but are both 'chairs.' They both share certain qualities that all chairs share– they possess a "chair-ness."

That as may be, argues Plato, but how do we *know* they're chairs? What *is* this "chair-ness"? We can sit on them, of course, but we can also sit on rocks, or sculptures, or the ground, and those things certainly aren't chairs. We can sit on them comfortably, we might proclaim– they're designed for human tushies. However, how does that explain your average airplane seats, which are, according to the evidence, typically designed by a panel of malevolent, misanthropic sea slugs after a night of heavy drinking? Well, they have a *look* to them: an arched back, a flat seat, and they're elevated off of the ground.

Yes, replies Plato, but *vide:*

---

[9]     http://www.incrediblediary.com/most-incredible-armchairs.html

That one doesn't even **look** like a chair, but these rubbery ball thingies are showing up in more and more offices every day.

And while we're on the subject, what about this thing? Yes, it **looks** like a chair, but....

If it looks like a chair, but you can't even sit in it, does it really count as a chair?

---

[10] "Pencil Chair" by German artist Kerstin Schulz. http://weburbanist.com/2009/10/11/oh-sit-the-worlds-13-most-uncomfortable-chair-designs/?ref=search

(I'm not even going to touch things like **this**):

In essence, what Plato was concerned about was the relationship between this:

And all of these, the results of a Google Image search for "chair":

[11]"Octopus Chair" by Maximo Riera. Source: http://www.curatedmag.com/news/2011/01/13/octopus-chair-by-maximo-riera/octo-chair-02-curatedmag/

I mean, we all kind of know what a chair is, but as soon as we try to pin down specifics, it gets really tricky. So how come we know what the chair is?

There must be, Plato posited, some kind of blueprint, or archetype, of CHAIR-- a Form that exists in an actual Ideal Realm, on which the various chairs in the universe are based. What's more, we must somehow have "access" to that realm; we must be able to come to an understanding of the archetype of CHAIR, and recall it whenever we see one of its less abstract variations down here in the World of Forms.

For Plato, this Ideal Realm included the blueprints for EVERYTHING. Every variant that exists of something here in the World of

Forms-- dogs, cats, bananas, parking meters, soufflés-- everything has a kind of behind-the-scenes model that provides the basis of its structure, from which it gets its dogginess, cattiness, bananainess, parking meteriness, and souffléiness.

If we *really* wanted to get crazy, we could go even further into the fact that these images are *representations* of chairs, and therefore even *further* from the Ideal Realm, but for now let's stick to the basics. Hopefully by now you have the idea. If you *are* interested in learning more about this subject, you should definitely read *The Symposium*, which also contains a lot of hilarious homoerotic banter, so there's that.

One other note: Plato believed that the Ideal Realms actually existed, and that these Ideals had substance. Whether or not this is the case is moot for this discussion, but this little idea is behind SO MUCH of Western thought that it's really a good theory to have rattling around in your brain. This is an incredibly cursory overview of an deeply enriching theory that becomes more fascinating and useful the better you know it. **Get to know Plato!**

So, back to the topic at hand: how does this discussion of chairs and Ideals help understand the Aeons? It helps because we can think of the Aeons as *the Ideal archetypes of positive abstract qualities*. If you read the excerpts from Gnostic literature above this post, you'll see the Aeons described as abstractions: Understanding, Memory, Perfection, Peace, Wisdom, etc. The Aeons within the Pleroma are the archetypes behind our limited ability to grasp abstractions.

Take Peace, for example. Here in the World of Forms, Peace can be peace between two people, or between two countries, or between two ears. It can be a still silence like a breeze on a cool day in the sun, or a loud movie you get to enjoy without the insanity of the daily struggle at work. Whatever the individual aspect here in the World of Forms, these experiences, to the Gnostics, are all modelled after the Aeon of PEACE.

Also, remember how I described the Ideals as "blueprints," on which lower forms were modelled? Well, in the Gnostic myth, the Demiurge and the Archons attempted to follow these blueprints when they created the World of Forms, but were looking beyond an abyss– the blueprints were all distorted and covered in coffee rings and ink stains. This is the whole reason for the (mythological) imperfection of this world we live in, and why we all *know* what perfect PEACE or perfect MEMORY or perfect PERCEPTION are, but, with a few exceptions, can't do anything more than brush up against the experience thereof. The components of the World of Forms are based on bad copies of the originals, so yes, there are some nice bits, but a lot is also awfully off-kilter.

A large component of the Gnostic Mysteries is the contemplative ascent of the individual through the Pleroma.[12] The further into the Pleroma you go, the more abstract the Aeons become (surely there's an aeon of ABSTRACTION, right?). Eventually, it starts to make perfect sense that they can be described as both beings and as locations; as abstract qualities, they represent limitations of aspects of the Unknown God, with "borders" of meaning and purpose. To the Gnostic, attaining the level of the Aeons is a

---

[12] See, for instance, the Mysteries of the Gnostic Ascent in my *A Gnostic Prayerbook*.

huge deal, because down here we can only know truth, but in the Pleroma, we can actually seek after TRUTH.

# 6. Pistis Sophia and the Creation of the Universe.

Of course, at some point, there has to be a differentiation between the Pleroma, that part of infinity which has been explored by the Aeons, and everything else: that part which has not. The part which has not is the Realm of Ignorance, also called the Outer Darkness; no knowledge yet exists of this realm in our tale.

Because the process unfolding within the Pleroma must include all possibilities, the possibility that one of the Aeons will try to explore the realm of ignorance without returning to the source also arises. Sophia, or Wisdom, a manifestation of Barbelo the Mother and the emanation farthest from the source of the Limitless Light, while hanging out at the border between the Pleroma and the Realm of Ignorance, has the desire to explore the Outer Darkness without returning to the Source (iterating). She does so in Good Faith (Pistis), but it's not necessarily the best idea.

Her desire to expand into the Outer Darkness without returning to the source results in the birth of the Demiurge, the Creator God of the World of Forms. Sophia's action thrusts him into the Outer Darkness. Within this Realm of Ignorance, the Demiurge and his assistants, the Archons, begin to ape the process of emanation which they can detect, imperfectly, within the realms above. They can't do it with material that's known to the Aeons, that has been "activated" through iteration; they have to do it with the dark, unknown gunk already in the Outer Darkness. This gunk is matter.

This all makes sense if you think about it. Gunk is currently what makes the world go 'round.

# 7. Chaos Theory and Gnostic Myth.

This mythology actually has parallels in mathematics. If you can stomach not-too-difficult math, fractal geometry works really well as a metaphor for the Gnostic creation myth. In chaos math, fractals are generated by way of iteration. As an example, suppose you have a system governed by the formula $x^2+1=y$, and begin the iterative process by giving x a value of 1. To iterate, you'd solve for y, and then replace x with your result for the next number. So, if x'=1, then our first y will be 2 — $(1)^2+1=2$. We'd then take x=2, and our new y is $(2)^2+1=5$. Our next would be $(5)^2+1=26$, etc. etc. Taking x and y as coordinates on a graph, you can map your iterations. In this case, it'd be a line that shoots to infinity to the upper right, no matter how many times the function is iterated. This is the way iterated systems are graphed. In this example, you have an ordered system, which wouldn't really represent what we all think of when we think of fractals.

Now, a fractal occurs when a seemingly random element is introduced into the system– essentially, when an integer is no longer whole. For example, let us take our $x^2+1=y$, but instead of starting at 1, we'll start at 1.081.

| x | y |
|---|---|
| 01.081 | 2.168561 |
| 2.168561 | 5.702656810721 |
| 5.702656810721 | 33.520294700862607220539841 |

Repeat this iteration about a million times and then restart with about a million different initial values, and you've got a fractal. This is why fractals weren't really discovered/developed until the modern era–you need a computer to repeat all of the millions of iterations needed to graph the fractal.

This is an important issue that goes largely unrecognized because of our habit of estimation and rounding when it comes to mathematics (our Good Faith in mathematics). It illustrates that a teensy, tiny alteration of a function way back at the beginning of the iterative process can cause radical change in the function later down the road. Suppose you're calculating air traffic control patterns based on records from the past ten years and you decide to round

1.00045 down to 1. Might make sense in the short term, but once that 1.00045 value kicks in down the road, you can be in serious trouble, as the results produced via the function deviate in the extreme from the predicted values.

So how does this fit in with Gnostic creation myth? As I mentioned above, the process of creation is described in Gnostic texts is an iterative process. The Limitless Light emanates two aspects, which return to the Limitless Light and emanate four aspects, and so forth. There is an equation here, which is a mystical variation on $y=x^2$, and every time a y variable is produced, it returns to the Limitless Light in order to continue the process.

Until, that is, we get to Sophia. Sophia emanates without returning to the Limitless Light– she runs the function without iterating– in essence, she estimates a value (in Good Faith/Pistis) instead of getting the proper value from the source. It's as though instead of iterating 15, she iterates 14.00036485. This produces a random element: the Demiurge, Yaldabaoth.

This random element added to the equation alters everything. Although the Demiurge and his initial creation were indeed slightly similar to the divine Aeons above, by the time it was iterated a gazillion times over, things got real freaky. When the Demiurge and the Archons created the Illusion that is the World of Forms, they were like the hapless air traffic controller who thought that rounding off numbers was a good idea. This produced an exceptionally "chaotic" universe, which may even be shaped and dictated by a chaotic function, which would explain everything from variations in red shift in astronomy to vibrational rates of movement in the Earth's crust to patterns in bird migration.

The Big Bang makes us think of a giant explosion that starts in a "center" and throws energy outward in relatively spherical radii, but the initial "bang" resulted in something that would look more like a 4-dimensional Mandelbrot set:

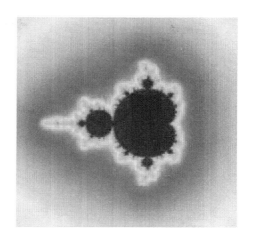

All fractals are self-similar, which means that all parts of any given fractal resemble the whole thing; because they're all governed by those initial equations, certain patterns have to manifest. It's like a coastline, which resembles itself on a map no matter the scale (a coastline from 1 mile up resembles a coastline from 100 feet) because it's all governed by connected patterns. So the rotation of the universe resembles the rotations of galaxies which resemble the rotations of solar systems, all the way down to the quantum level. Now, they may seem to be different, but the underlying initial structures at the very beginning of the iterative process are pretty much the same. Thus, we really did come about in God's image, as did the entire universe, though it doesn't sometimes look that way. It doesn't sometimes look that way because the Demiurge and the Archons want to stay in control, so they created the World of Forms in order to fool us.

## 8. The Demiurge.

Since the beginning of its conceptualization, no character in Gnostic mythology has been more divisive than the Demiurge, Yaldabaoth, Saklas, "Jehovah." The theory of an imperfect, intermediary deity who participated in the act of creation-- a deity often described in derogatory terms-- isn't the easiest conceit to discuss within the context of monotheism, even though the Gnostic idea of God definitely fits the bill. There **is** only One God, it's just that some of us have the wrong idea about which God is the One. This makes for some uncomfortable discussions when you go around talking about, for instance, the Demiurge described in the theology of $2^{nd}$ Century quasi-Gnostic bishop Marcion of Sinope, who considered Yaldabaoth basically one-to-one with the wrathful God of Genesis/Exodus/etc. (therefore, per Marcion of Sinope, the Judaic scriptures should be rejected).

Granted, Marcion's interpretation was more nuanced, and can be reconciled with acceptance of mystical Judaism, but misinterpretation of ideas like Marcion's leads to some serious anti-Semitic nastiness (Google "Gnostic Liberation Front" if you want an example– I don't want to send anyone to such an odious site by providing a link). Still, it's hard to tell people, "oh, you know that story you heard about Adam and Eve and whatnot? Well IT'S ALL WRONG, SUCKAS!" and have them get your meaning. I see this a lot in "Gnostic Gnewbies" who are in it for the shock value and don't care what other people think–– more on that in a moment–– but more mature individuals should note, with some concern, that **most people don't like being told that their most essential beliefs are wrong.** The whole "Demiurge" concept does just that, so how do we mitigate the noise when we're trying to talk about Yaldy-baldy? We do so by **trying to understand what we're talking about, and how best to communicate that concept to other people.**

First of all, let's go ahead and address Dumbo (he's right behind you!). Is the Demiurge a literal dude with a flowy white beard, sitting up there, in charge of either a cabal of nasty angels or (according to some of the more ridiculous silliness out there) a fleet of UFOs? Question for you: doesn't interpreting him this way result in the same errors of reason that crop up when Biblical literalists are all like, *"But God didn't create Adam and STEEEEEEEVE!"* (Answer: yes, yes it does.)

So what, then, is this Demiurge? Clearly, ideas about the interpretation of mythology in the First Century were a little different than they are now, and it's naive to think that, among the ancient Gnostics, there weren't a few who believed in a literal White-Robed Beardo in the Sky. But, given the modern context here, and the need to approach the material in the spirit of Reason, let me propose an alternative understanding of the Demiurge based on the myth and its utility in our day-to-day lives.

What do we know about the character of the Demiurge from the stories?

- The Demiurge isn't the Ultimate God, but thinks he is.
- The Demiurge was spawned from Wisdom (Sophia), but from Wisdom applied incorrectly (she screwed up).

- The Demiurge, via the creation of the Archons, is in charge of the way we perceive reality.
- The way we perceive reality is imperfect.
- The Demiurge wants us to worship him, and keeps us from understanding the True God/Pleroma.

Given these premises, what can we come up with as a definition of the Demiurge as an internal process? How about:

**The Demiurge is a false and irrational Image that we construct of the relationship between the Self and God based on our imperfect knowledge of the World of Forms.**

What does this mean? It means that since we're stuck here in the realms of imperfection, it's impossible for us to really conceptualize what we mean by "God." So, we create an Image of God that we worship in its stead. This Image may be derived from following precepts taught by a religion. It may be socio-cultural and learned. It may be completely self-derived. It's, however, inescapable– we all have a little Demiurge in us, judging us, asking us to judge others. It's not an external guy on a cloud or another planet; *the relationship between an individual and the Demiurge is just as personal as the relationship between an individual and God.*

The Demiurge resides in every person in the same sense that Sophia and the Christos reside in every person. **It's simply a matter of degree**. When an individual castigates another for an accident of the World of Forms (for example, when someone is racist or bigoted), they're "worshiping the Demiurge," as they're acting upon impulses which are clearly based on images they have of what "should" or "shouldn't" be. When a person negatively judges based on an image she has created, she's giving Yaldabaoth a nod. When, however, **that very same person** commits an act of kindness, compassion or love, they're worshipping the true, Unknown God of Sophia and the Christos.

The Demiurge isn't a concept that can readily be applied to an entire religion. **Some** aspects of **all** religions are Demiurgic, when they support the judgement of individuals based on legalistic proscription. **Some** aspects of **all** religions are also, however, Sophianic, and representative of the true spiritual path we recognize as gnosis. For every Crusades (Demiurgic), we have a Catholic Social Services (Sophianic). For every Tomas de Torquemada, we have a St. Francis of Assisi.

**Gnostics can worship the Demiurge, too**. Some Gnostic scripture contains legalism and judgement on others based on images. Some Gnostics are terribly anti-Judaic and elitist. Some modern so-called "Gnostics" use Gnostic mythology as an excuse for anti-Semitism or cultism or guruism.

This Way implies, "Don't worship the Demiurge." This doesn't, however, mean that one should abandon one's spiritual Path, **even if that spiritual Path is "mainstream."** What we mean by "Don't worship the Demiurge" is "Don't worship false images." Don't judge people unduly. Don't put words into God's mouth. *Don't be a jerk*.

In the interest of Not Being a Jerk, now is also probably a good time to talk about something I've termed **the Anarchonic Fallacy.** This is a big one, especially among people new to the Gnostic scene, who get there via the Matrix or Elaine Pagels' woefully out-of-date *Gnostic Gospels*. The Anarchonic Fallacy states that, since Gnostic myth often depicts The Demiurge/Creator God and the Archons in opposition to the True God, *our singular duty is to 'freak out the squares.'*

Those under the spell of the Anarchonic Fallacy take the Gnostic myths as fundamentally literal as Bible-believing Christians take the story of the Flood. They believe that the purpose of the Gnostic Way is to *rebel*, that established institutions such as churches or political systems are *no good*, that the Gnostic can and should be anything she wants to be, by gum, because Nobody Can Tell Us What To Do. We see this a lot in people who think the Demiurge is controlling some Archons who control the Government/Church, therefore there is a *conspiracy of UFO aliens in charge of The President's Head and We Should Fight Them YEAH!*

The problem with the Anarchonic Fallacy is, as I see it, three-fold. First, it depends upon the *literal* understanding of the Demiurge we talked about upstairs, i.e. there is a half-lion, half-serpent flying around in the sky directing his sinister Archons who, in turn, direct all the bad that occurs in the world.

The second problem with the Anarchonic Fallacy is that it depends upon ideas about the Gnostics that were spread by early opponents of the movement, polemicists such as Irenaeus of Lyons. This is far from surprising; until the 1970's, 9/10ths of the information we had about the Gnostics came from their enemies. Apart from some fragmented texts and the almost unread *Pistis Sophia*, if you wanted to study the Gnostics before 1974 and you weren't a student of the Coptic language, you read the Church Fathers. The Church Fathers were opposed to philosophies that didn't mesh with their own— *- a perfectly reasonable stance for Church Fathers to take--* and therefore played more than a bit loose with their rhetoric and arguments. Now, however, that we have the Nag Hammadi texts, we're coming to understand that the practices of our Alexandrian and Syrian and Chaldaen and Roman forebears was far more complex and nuanced than those portrayed by Irenaeus et al., so it damned well better be nuanced for us, too. It's not as cut-and-dry as "GNOSTIC VERSUS DEMIURGE" or "WE GOOD, THEY BAD."

Which brings us to the third, and most serious problem with the Anarchonic Fallacy: **it completely misses the point because it doesn't go far enough**. Gnostic myth does, undoubtedly, caution us against placing faith in worldly control structures. It counsels us to rebel against the Demiurge, that Wrathful Face of God created by human misconception, and his Archons, Fear and Terror and Blind Obedience, the Planetary Powers, et al. It does tell us to laugh in the face of authority and to cast down worldly things. It does contradict much of the doctrine of the early orthodoxy and the mainstream churches as they've developed today. I'm personally even fond of referring to the Gnostics as the "original anarchists."

***But, this is only a Tiny Fraction of the Gnostic Story.***

The point behind tearing down these structures, behind admonishing the control systems and demolishing the illusion of the world is to Rebuild It For The Pleroma. This

Way isn't about hatred or violence or the rebellion of the sullen teenaged soul who is tired of being Told What To Do. It's about THIS, from the Valentinian *Gospel of Truth (NHL)*:

> Speak concerning the truth to those who seek it and of knowledge to those who, in their error, have committed sin. Make sure-footed those who stumble and stretch forth your hands to the sick. Nourish the hungry and set at ease those who are troubled. Foster men who love. Raise up and awaken those who sleep. For you are this understanding which encourages. If the strong follow this course, they're even stronger.

Nor is it about casting away Faith, another common trope of the Anarchonic Fallacy, that faith is somehow stupid and gnosis is *where it's at*. It's about THIS, from *The Gospel of Philip (NHL:*

> Faith receives, love gives. No one will be able to receive without faith. No one

will be able to give without love. Because of this, in order that we may indeed receive, we believe, and in order that we may love, we give, since if one gives without love, he has no profit from what he has given.

Nor is it about "freaking out the squares," so commonly embraced by those under the sway of the Anarchonic Fallacy. This Way was never about telling people how wrong they're, no matter how canonical or mainstream. This Way is a path of kindness and love for ALL beings. This Way is a Way of Compassion. It's about THIS, from *The Dialogue of the Saviour* (NHL):

> Judas said, "Tell me, Lord, what the beginning of the path is." [Jesus] said, "Love and goodness. For if one of these existed among the Archons, wickedness would never have come into existence."

Finally-- and to me this is the saddest thing about the Anarchonic Fallacy-- *it stops short of gnosis itself.* Gnosis isn't just a mystical experience. It's personal acquaintance with divinity as tempered by Wisdom and Reason. There's nothing there about hating the world and rebelling against it; it's about cultivating an experiential attitude in which the world itself opens its gates to the inbreaking fullness of God, the Limitless Light that exists beyond individuation. It's not equally applicable to people or organizations we simply like or dislike. It's an experience that needs to be had to understood within its own context, and all of this rebellion is just so much distraction from the PERSONAL path. Gnosis is about YOU, not about what other people are up to!

As the Demiurge is such a personal concept, and as the danger exists that overly focusing on him will lead to the Anarchonic Fallacy, we can see that claiming that such-and-such a religion or such-and-such a caste or such-and-such a political body consists of people worshiping the Demiurge commits the fallacy of hasty generalization. Judging an entire body of persons based upon what may be a single aspect of a single individual one has encountered is pretty irrational.

We tend to base our judgments on experience; those who claim that this or that is "Demiurgic" usually qualify this judgement by pointing to examples from the media or people they have met. The problem with this approach is that one casts aspersions onto millions of people based on one's experiences with a handful of representatives of these belief systems. Judging the interior spiritual life of millions of people based on a handful of examples, **no matter how extreme the examples**, is an irrational act. **So, claiming that people who are not Gnostics are worshippers of the Demiurge is in and of itself a Demiurgic Act**. It's the creation of an interpretation of a reality based on the imperfect information of the World of Forms.

Don't **be** the Demiurge. **Conquer** it. Don't fall into the Anarchonic fallacy. Instead, try to use Sophia and the Logos, your inner Wisdom and Reason, to cut through the easy bullshit being spouted by the Yaldabaoth in your mind.

# 9. The Archons.

The Archons represent impelled systems. To the Sethians, these systems were astrological; astrology is a good short-hand for Archonic forces because according to the understanding of astrology in the ancient world, it was governed by **fate.** Allow me to quote at length from *This Way*:

> Mythically, the Sethians were very concerned with what we refer to as "escaping astral determinism." This is the idea of escaping from "heimarmene," or fate, by recognizing and denying the influence of the astrological Archons on one's existence in the World of Forms. In the Books of the Saviour (*Pistis Sophia*), we find entire passages which discuss the Christos' ascent through the Planetary Spheres, during which he "changes the direction" of the Spheres, thereby ruining the ability of astrologers to divine:

...[T]hou hast taken their power from them and from their horoscope-casters and their consulters and from those who declare to the men in the world all things which shall come to pass, in order that they should no more from this hour know how to declare unto them any thing at all which will come to pass.

At a later point in the codice, in a different book in the same collection, the soul of the Knower, ascending through these Spheres, delivers a resounding denial to the Rulers of Fate who would subject it to Destiny:

Take your destiny! I come not to your regions from this moment onwards. I have become a stranger unto you for ever, being about to go unto the region of my inheritance.

Another, similar account in which the Spheres are disturbed, thereby eliminating Fate can be found in the text "Trimorphic Protennoia":

> And the lots of Fate and those who apportion the domiciles were greatly disturbed over a great thunder. And the thrones of the Powers were disturbed, since they were overturned, and their King was afraid. And those who pursue Fate paid their allotment of visits to the path, and they said to the Powers, "What is this disturbance and this shaking that has come upon us through a Voice to the exalted Speech? And our entire habitation has been shaken, and the entire circuit of the path of ascent has met with destruction, and the path upon which we go, which takes us up to the Archgenitor of our birth, has ceased to be established for us."

That sacramental practice could unloose the bonds of Fate is attested to in the "Excerpts of Theodotus," a collection of Valentinian sayings recorded by Clement of Alexandria:

> Until baptism, they say, Fate is effective, but after it the astrologers no longer speak the truth. Isn't the bath alone that makes us free, but also the knowledge: who were we? what have we become? where were we? into what place have we been cast? whither are we hastening? from what are we delivered? what is birth? what is rebirth?

Again and again we find this concept in the literature. The human is trapped within the World of Forms, under the subject of the Archons, who rule the Zodiac and the Planetary Spheres. This lack of control over one's own set of circumstances leads to what we refer to in Way-speak as the "Kenomic Worldview."

Modern prophet Philip K. Dick also discusses an escape from astral determinism in the *Tractates Cryptica Scriptura*:

> 49. Two realms there are, upper and lower. The upper, derived from hyperuniverse I or Yang, Form I of Parmenides, is sentient and volitional. The lower realm, or Yin, Form II of Parmenides, is mechanical, driven by blind, efficient cause, deterministic and without intelligence, since it emanates from a dead source. In ancient times it was termed 'astral determinism.' We are trapped, by and large, in the lower realm, but are through the sacraments, by means of the plasmate, extricated. Until astral determinism is broken, we are not even aware of it, so occluded

are we. 'The Empire never ended.'

As PKD says, until we break this astral determinism, we are so under its influence that we don't even recognize it. Through various ascent practices, represented in this Way by the Greater Precepts or Renunciation of the Archons, we begin to recognize that we exist in this state, and may begin to address it. In essence, we begin to recognize that the Archons are themselves imperfect, and depending upon their influences as guides for Right Action will only ever have imperfect results. This is why we disregard what horoscope casters have to say, and use divinatory tools such as tarot cards as intended– as tools for self-discovery, not for determining future paths.[13]

---

[13] *This Way: Gnosis Without Gnosticism.* Jeremy Puma, 2011.

Writ a bit smaller, these impelled systems, symbolized by-- and discussed in terms of-- astrological associations, are directed by both the individual, and by external organizations which intend to establish some kind of control over each one of us. Within the individual (psychologically), the Archons can manifest as the Masks of the Demiurge. Within the external World (hypostatically), the Archons can manifest as Masks of Collective Societal Assumptions. **They (and the Aeons) can also manifest as the inexplicable ("supernatural" or "occult").** This is a subject we'll be touching upon in more detail at a later time.

As the servants of the Demiurge, the Archons carry out his wishes in the form of systems which stimulate human passions, especially that of fear, through which it's exceptionally easy to establish control. **It's a huge mistake to think that any single organization ("the Church," "Government," "The X Political Party") is Demiurgic or Archonic.** As we explained before, **all** human organizations have the capacity to act Demiurgically. Often, the organizations that speak out the loudest against what we might consider "Archonic" are just as infected as the more obvious instances.

I want to repeat that: **It's a huge mistake to think that any single organization ("the Church," "Government," "The X Political Party") is Demiurgic or Archonic.**

Ok, so, as image-creating denizens of an imperfect Universe, we are direly susceptible to control by the Demiurge and the Archonic entities under his wings. We read in the *Dialogue of the Saviour* (NHL) that, **"Truly, fear is the power [of the Rulers]. So if you are going to be afraid of what is about to come upon you, it will engulf you."** In Gnostic mythology, the Archons have been using this fear as a control method since the very beginning. As the Dragon Yaldabaoth and the Archons desire to maintain control over the world in which we live, they do so through the rule of Fear, letting us scare ourselves into submission with illusory threats and vacant horrors.

**The easiest way to recognize the works of the Archons is by noticing**

**whether they're intended to instil a sense of fear in someone in order to control that person.** That said, fear isn't their only modus operandi, not by a long stretch. It's just the **best place for beginning Archon-hunters to look.**

The Archons work in words, in semiotics and semantics. In this way, they're master propagandists, and we may find evidence of their scriptural tampering in places within scripture which are completely driven by control systems. Whether a Gnostic scribe was possessed by an 'evil spirit' or his or her own personal legalistic beliefs, we can't rule out that this process influenced the scribe's hand when composing individual verses within scripture. Sectarianism or subservience to Archonic urges– these are two possible masks worn by the scribe that result in what we might call "**The Demiurgic Verses**" in both Gnostic and Canonical literature.

We can avoid the impelled systems of the Archons by embracing the Logos and Sophia—Divine Reason, who manifested within Jesus Christ, and Wisdom, the feminine aspect of the Limitless Light who both birthed the Demiurge and saves us from him. In practice, this means **cultivating our own gnosis**, self-knowledge, and learning to recognize impelled systems for what they are. **Gnosis is literally the knowledge that saves us from the Archons.** Of course, this approach also means **avoiding the practice of expecting others to conform to our idea of reality, even those who are obviously acting under the influence of the Demiurge.**

We can avoid the Archons by cultivating compassion for all conscious beings trapped within this World of Forms, including those with whom we disagree. We can also avoid the Archons by living humbly and relating to those around us with love and assistance.

# 10. An Aside: Hypostatic versus Psychological.

The question is, are the Aeons and the Archons **REALLY REAL**? Do they exist in manifest nature, palpable within the World of Forms? Can they, theoretically, be perceived using the senses? For clarity, let's call this position "Hypostatic" (more on this term in a moment). Or, are they psychological metaphors? Are they mental constructs or Jungian symbols that point towards internal facets of the human psyche? Let's call this position "Psychological." We find the full spectrum in the current wave of Gnostic thought, from the pure mentation of neo-Jungians to the "Archons=Aliens!" silliness of Samael Aon Weor and John Lamb Lash. There are obvious problems with both approaches.

The problem with the hypostatic approach is that isn't currently *de rigour* to take spiritual information literally. Make no mistake; although many neognostics like to claim otherwise, many of the original Gnostic sects most certainly believed in the literal existence of the Archons (otherwise, why title a book "ON THE REALITY OF THE ARCHONS"?).

Literalism can certainly be dangerous, but, in our modern culture, beset by adherents of the Anarchonic Fallacy, it's also unhip. Nobody into modern spirituality wants to "take the Bible literally," because a whole bunch of people did so in the past and terrible things came about. As an example, take a recent story of a snake handler pastor who died after being bitten by a rattler at a church service. Read any article on the subject, and you'll find comment after comment stating stuff like "Looks like Darwin was right!" or "That's what he gets!" or whatever. These pathological comments are defended by arguments that those who take the Bible literally (in this case, Mark 16:17-18) somehow "deserves" a painful death.

However, anyone familiar with these sects knows that they generally consist of kind, peace-loving people who just want to be left alone to worship as they see fit. In point of fact, many of the serpent-handling congregations in the South were pioneers of integration, and welcomed all races to their services, as the proper Christian thing to do.

And if you don't think the ancient Gnostics themselves engaged in a little literal serpent-handling, you should study the material a little better.

Snake-handling aside, some literalism is, of course, ridiculous. Replacing evolution with creationism in school textbooks, using Leviticus for persecution of minorities, etc. etc. etc. That being said, can't it be argued that a certain amount of literalism is actually good? For instance, let's suppose someone literally followed the Sermon on the Mount. Would the same commenters who bashed the snake-handler for taking the Bible literally also bash someone who takes the Bible so literally that she literally enacts the Works of Mercy?

So let's table this question for a moment and investigate the psychological position. This position seems to be championed by Jungian neognostics like Stephen Hoeller, who have glommed onto the work of Carl Jung (Jung was, of course, an anti-Semite, but that's neither here nor there at the moment). Jung had a famous interest in "Gnosticism," and many of his ideas have been transformed by popular culture, projected backwards onto the ancient Gnostics as though they were a bunch of primitive psychoanalysts.

This kind of backwards projection can be as dangerous as literalism; most of the nasty myths used to support some of the nastiest of human activities are due to this tendency we have to project our own interpretation of reality onto those who have preceded us. The ancient Gnostics, the Medieval alchemists, the Cathars, the Knights Templar, etc., were not depth psychologists. That being said, the Aeons and Archons and processes described by the Gnostics are almost perfect as metaphorical vehicles for self-discovery. There are some excellent reasons to use Gnostic myth to investigate one's nature on a purely psychological level.

However! We live in a crazy place where weird stuff happens all the time! To claim that there are no super- or supranatural intelligences that occasionally interfere in human society is to ignore entire mountains of evidence. As a dedicated Fortean, I've experienced events that, to me, demonstrate that there are "intelligences" within the World of Forms that have their own modus operandi, intelligences that we are not generally meant to understand (vide also the works of Jacques Vallee and John Keel). There is enough of a religious element in inexplicable events that occur to this day to convince me that there are actual Aeons and Archons who involve themselves in our world. But doesn't that make me a crazy literalist?

So, how do we reconcile the hypostatic and psychological? Is it possible to hold both viewpoints at the same time without going insane? I posit that there is indeed a way to do so, if one accepts a Phildickian approach, and understands the entities described in the Gnostic myth cycle as, in fact, Living Information. We are Information Processors. Information can arrive via the external senses (hypostatic), or it can arrive through our internal (psychological) processes. Living Information can dwell within us as what Dick termed a "plasmate," awakened when we receive gnosis, but can also dwell externally, in the World of Forms. It can manifest as a quality that influences the way we make decisions or understand our own impulses, or it can manifest as a strange ball of light in the sky or a nasty horror from the Outer

Darkness. It can manifest as a sudden flash of realization about the nature of God, or it can manifest as a brightly robed Luminary (angels are, of course, "Messengers," or bearers of information).

If these powers are Living Information, where did that Information come from? Well, a spiritual Way has to have some Mysteries, doesn't it?

Information stands across the gap between the literal and the metaphorical. But, here's another thing about it: everyone perceives it differently. The Aeons and Archons are, we could say, bundles of Living Information with similar characteristics that can be perceived by denizens of the World of Forms. The question of good literalism versus bad literalism then becomes a different issue: what do we choose to do with these bundles?

Inspired by the Living Information contained in the New Testament to feed the poor? **Boom: Psychological, Aeonic.**

Inspired by the Living Information contained in the Old Testament to hate on gays? **Boom: Psychological, Archonic.**

Living Information in the form of a scary UFO/angel tell you that the world is going to end and you should persecute nonbelievers, so you do? Boom: **Hypostatic, Archonic.**

Living Information in the form of a Christ-like figure who tells you to be nice to people? **Boom: Hypostatic, Aeonic.**

It's all about what you do with something that happens to you.

## 11. The World of Forms and the Black Iron Prison.

I prefer to think of the universe we live in as the "World of Forms," though it might more accurate to call it the "World of Manifested Forms." The "Forms," in this case, are the things we interact with using our senses—anything that can be seen, heard, smelled, touched or tasted (or 'sensed' using extra-physical perception).

There can no doubt that we consider the World of Forms a creation of the Demiurge, but this is a nuanced concept. The Demiurge himself is the ultimate illusion, and his creations are already "redeemed" in a timeless fashion. In other words, if you consider the events of the totality of existence in terms of the infinity represented by the Limitless Light, things all work out well enough in the end.

So, we might be tempted to think of matter as "evil," though a better term might be *imperfect*, or at worst *insane*, because it's a reflection of Ultimate Reality. A good way to describe this idea is **"mitigated dualism."** Down here in the World of Forms, matter and spirit are completely separate, and never the twain shall meet. In the realms above the World of Forms, however, things are a little more complex.

"Materiality" as a concept only exists within the illusory World of Forms, within those of us who choose to try to exercise power instead of participating in the emergence of the Limitless Light. When we view causality as an enemy or something to be conquered or controlled, it becomes an enemy. **When, however, we awaken to the realization that we all contain the seed of the Living God, we begin to understand that the Christos and Sophia are always available to us, and that this realm can be transcended.** This awakening means casting off the shackles placed upon us by the Archons in the Black Iron Prison.

Let's talk about the World of Forms, and the implications of living in an illusory world. What does it mean, to say "**Reality isn't real, man!**" I mean, **beyond the hackneyed clichés of devotees of the Matrix films, does "This world is an illusion!" really mean anything at all?** Let's be frank: I get hungry, I need to eat, and sushi is *delicious*. This doesn't seem like an illusion– neither does hitting my thumb with a hammer when I'm building a spice rack. The idea can even be insulting and morally distasteful if you carry it out to its extreme *a la* the purveyors of *The Secret* and the "you create your own reality" morons. **"Don't worry, starving Nicaraguan orphan– the world is an Illusion! All you have to do is *think real hard* about food and it'll magically appear for you!"** So how can we say "The World is an Illusion" and give it some kind of value?

As sensual beings, we can only experience and perceive those aspects of the World of Forms which are available to our senses (sight, hearing, scent, touch and taste, plus any additional hoodoo you'd like to include). We generally assume that the more senses with which we directly perceive something, the truer or more valid our experience is. For the most part, this is true. For instance, climbing a mountain is a valid experience which requires utilization of all available senses. Watching a movie about climbing a mountain is less valid–– one uses only the senses of hearing and sight. Looking at a picture of a mountaintop is even less valid than that-- only sight is required.

This generally accepted view of experience has some tragic flaws. For instance, what about books? They typically only "require" sight. But, isn't the novel *The Return of the King* more "valid" than the film version? Or, what about music? We generally only hear it. But, unequivocally, listening to Beethoven's 9th Symphony is far more "real" an experience to music lovers than watching the latest episode of "American Idol," for which one would have to utilize both hearing and sight. Or, even more confusing, is a painting of a vase of daises by Van Gogh more or less real than a photograph of a vase of daisies in a newspaper advertisement for vases? How about the experience of seeing a star, the light of which took ten thousand years to reach us, knowing that the star might have since exploded in a supernova? Are we really viewing the light of the star?

**So, the accepted definition of valid experience as something that is specifically sensual isn't so cut-and-dry.** The missing component is **personal engagement**, or internal interaction. With this added to the mix, we have a different story altogether. **Valid experience must include personal engagement**. The experience must speak to the individual on a personal level based on that individual's epistemological engagement with what is being perceived. Something is truly only "real," or valid, to whomever is experiencing it if the experience includes all available senses and engagement, or internal interaction, with whatever is being experienced.

Without engagement, an experience can never truly be valid. Why? **Because as humans, we define reality based on what engages us personally.** If something doesn't truly engage us, we tend to write it out of our personal realities. This is why learning based on testing and lectures and rote simply can't work across the board; without the component of personal engagement, the information being presented is literally unreal to the bored student. **Based on our definition of valid experience, we find that engagement with perception is what forms our reality as we interact with the World of Forms; without experience and**

**engagement, we are walking through a world of images.**

Compounding the matter is the issue of memory and the role it plays in experience. In fact, it can be convincingly argued that **all that we experience is the memory of a thing**. If this is the case, our perceptions and experiences are based on structures within the brain, and our realities are based on remembered images. The more valid an experience, the more likely one is to remember it. Consequently, valid experiences constitute reality.

Now, it must be remembered that "valid" and "invalid" come without value judgements. **For instance, a psychopathic murderer can have a valid experience while disembowelling a victim. A heart surgeon can have an invalid experience while saving someone's life.** We're simply talking about levels of perceiving reality at this point, not good or evil or morality or ethics.

Up until now, we've focused on subjective experience, or personal experience-- that which makes the World of Forms real to the individual. **But, what about collective**

**experience?** Is objectivity possible? If you climb a mountain with a friend, and it engages you but doesn't engage him, is that mountain still "real"? It would be absurd to fall into the trap of denying that external reality exists. We can deny its reality all we want, even if it doesn't engage us, but if we toss ourselves off of a mountain, we'll soon find out how objectively "real" it is. **The World of Forms certainly exists**, **as such, full of solidity and heavy stuff that falls on peoples' heads.** It's the **interaction** of the subjective and the objective that now begins to concern us.

You may have heard the parable of the Blind Men and the Elephant before. In fact, you've probably heard it a Real Lot. But guess what: **I'm going to trot out that sucker again.** Some tools are worth keeping around, even when they're old.

> The buddha brought four blind men into a room with an elephant and asked them what the elephant was. The first blind man touched the elephant's leg and claimed, "the elephant is a pillar. It's cylindrical and firm to the

touch." The second man touched the elephant's flank. "nonsense," he said, "this elephant is no pillar. It's a wall—firm and smooth and large!" The third blind man felt the elephant's ear. "you are both wrong—this elephant isn't a pillar or a wall. Rather, it's some kind of flag, not firm at all, but waving back and forth in the wind." Finally, the last blind man grabbed the elephant's tail. "you are all stupid as well as blind," he said. "this elephant is obviously nothing more than a small section of rope."

Although this parable is used most often to preach tolerance for other points of view, it carries a deeper meaning for our conversation. The elephant exists, objectively. **It exists, however, as four different items to the four blind men.** For the purposes of our discussion, let's remove the Buddha from the picture. The Blind Men are alone with the elephant. Now suppose they combine their observations. Is it more likely that they'd come up with the elephant? Or, is it more likely that they'd think they were in a room with four separate objects? **Perhaps one of the blind men is stronger than the others, and he kills them and declares that, since nobody opposes his observation any longer, the elephant is damn well a wall AND YOU'D BETTER GO ALONG, BUB!**

Or, let's suppose that they combine their observations and the **do** decide that they're in a room with an elephant. Would any of them **really** have an idea of what an elephant is at its very essence? Without the Buddha to tell them so, would the elephant have the same objective reality to the blind men as it would to a zoologist? The answer, of course, is no, **don't be crazy.** Instead, each man would have an image in his head about what exactly that elephant was. All four images would be designed based on each man's experience. Each image would be different (perhaps radically so).

Now, let's suppose that through experience and engagement, the men spent some time learning more about the elephant. Let's suppose they really cared to find out, and took measurements, drew diagrams, climbed the elephant, fed it, smelled its poo, dissected it and made crafts from its carcass. Would the men **then** have the same objective reality to the men as it would to a zoologist? **Again, no.** They'd have a more valid experience of the elephant, but without the actual experience of the zoologist, they'd have a completely different picture of the beast. Their knowledge of the beast would be based on internal images created by their more valid experiences.

And this is the crux of the matter. **This separation between subjectivity and objectivity leads us to create images in our minds based on perception and experience that are not actually representative of the World of Forms.** In other words, **our realities based on valid and invalid experiences create an image of the world within each of us that is an unreal image. And this is what we mean when we say that the World of Forms, the world, is an illusion**. We don't mean it's some transparent projection or mirage that you can put your hand through. We mean that **this is the hallucination each of us experience**. Essentially, the only way to know reality in a non-illusory fashion is to have a valid experience of all of reality, all at the same time-- to **be**, and to engage with, **everything simultaneously**.

Obviously, as conscious beings who can interact with our fellows, we can adjust to our perceptual limitations, at least inasmuch as our societies tend to function. We all know, for instance, that the Sun "rises" in the morning and "sets" at night, that current events are reported in such-and-such a fashion, that we work in this or that place, etc. etc. We have enough of a perceptive ability to come up with a generally agreed-upon version of "reality" as far as the basic functions go. **Or, so we think**.

Let's come back to the Elephant for a sec. Suppose that, instead of the Buddha, the blind men are in the room with the elephant and Genghis Khan. And, let's suppose that Genghis needs the blind men to work in his army, hauling stuff around for his soldiers. Genghis pokes the elephant with a pointy stick, and the beast emits a loud trumpet which scares the heck out of the blind men. **"Terrible, isn't it?"** asks Genghis. **"It's a dangerous devil beast with the power to destroy buildings and crush the life out of you! I can protect you from it, but I need** armies to do so. Come toil for me, and we'll wipe these hideous monsters from the face of the Earth!"

Old Genghis used the **fear** the men experienced from the noise, **a valid experience for them due to engagement**, to create a **false reality** in which **all elephants must be destroyed**. The false reality is based on invalid experience, of course, but **the men confused the experience of the fear with the false experience of Genghis Khan's tall tale, so they're duped into believing that the illusory image of the "devil beast" is "real."**

There are forces in the world that recognize the illusion, this general insanity of the World of Forms. These forces seek to control the World of Forms for one reason or another. So, taking advantage of our inability to discern reality, they seek to shape our realities for us via **control systems**. These systems are generally intricate webs or networks of invalid experiences designed to control the illusions or hallucinations of individuals, in order to further the goals of whomever designed the system.

The key characteristic of a Control System is that it dupes its victims into confusing valid and invalid experiences. Take, for instance, advertising. Advertisers and marketers have one goal: to get their target audiences to say "yes" to an advertised product. To do so, they employ a whole bag of tricks that can create valid experiences within said audiences, tricks that play on the illusory nature of experience.

As a better example, take a look at government. Based on our analysis of valid versus invalid experiences, and our discussion about the elephant and the blind men, **just how "real" is democracy**? Isn't it nothing more than a giant control system, which by its very nature seeks only its own survival through the medium of control? **The control structure is ingrained through the creation of false engagement by those who seek to perpetuate their structures**.

Philip Dick called the entire network of control structures in which we reside the "Black Iron Prison." The B.I.P. is the ultimate illusion, because it not only dupes the individual into believing that invalid experiences are valid, but it also creates a false structure within the experiences and memory of the individual.

Although one would think that it's vice-versa, the further removed from the center of valid experience one is, the more effective the control system. Those who don't seek out more valid experiences of society are more easily ensnared by the Black Iron Prison, which gladly supplies "valid experiences" for those who need them. The goal of each one of us is to break free of the Black Iron Prison and have as many valid experiences as possible. **This breaking free is what we refer to as *gnosis*.**

## 12. Gnosis.

Hypostatically, the upshot of this whole process is that the Limitless Light's self-knowledge has been interrupted within the realm of ignorance by the Demiurge, who wants us to worship him. Sophia realized this immediately, of course, which is one of the reasons she gets called Wisdom, and set about correcting this error by essentially sneaking a portion of the Limitless Light into the human-being assembly line. With the Logos, she activates that portion of the Limitless Light within us, allowing us to understand who we are, where we come from, where we are and where we are going. This activation by both the Logos and Sophia is called *gnosis*.

Even a cursory glance through the extant material illustrates that the word "gnosis" doesn't mean what most people say it means. It's not anything like "enlightenment" in the popular sense of the word. It's not some kind of radical insight granted by taking entheogens. It's a multi-faceted understanding that has multiple components, which we describe, in *This Way*, as a formula: Gnosis = Awakening (Word + Wisdom).

Gnosis includes:

**A: An Awakening Event** – This might be an epiphany, a theophany, a revelation, etc., but it must be personal and must be experienced. Way persons may participate in and perform the Christian Sacrament of the Eucharist, and perform and recognize the validity of the other Christian Sacraments. The primary practice for the cultivation of awakening, however, is contemplative.

**L: The Word, or Logos** – An informational context into which one can place the awakening event. Remember that one of the meanings of Logos is "word," but it also means "faculty of reason," "discourse," "law," "pronouncement." Jesus Christ, as the Logos, represents the deliverer of discourse– in Buddhist terms, we may find similarities to the Buddha as the Living Dharma. In the Sethian myth, Jesus carries forth the Discourse as an extended faculty of reason initiated in the Pleroma by the Divine Seth. The preexistent Logos within the Pleroma is the Christos, which manifests within the World of Forms as living information. He's the instructor who institutes the sacraments: information. He teaches the Way to his disciples: information. He facilitates the presence of the Nous within each of us: information.

**S: Wisdom, or Sophia** – The wisdom to apply the awakening event through action within one's holistic life. This is Sophia, tempered by faith, who carries us forward in our day-to-day existence. She delivers the essential Wisdom necessary to apply the teachings of the Logos to day-to-day life. With her infinite compassion, she descends through the spheres of the Archons to engage the spirit in each of us and allow us to develop compassion for all beings. She allows us to perform the sacraments presented by the Logos wisely, and fills our actions with content, keeping us moving forward and upward as we climb the ladder of emanations towards the realms of the Pleroma.

If it doesn't include all three of these components, it might be pretty cool, but it ain't gnosis.

Something else: gnosis doesn't give you superpowers, the ability to read minds or materialize things out of thin air. It isn't available for sale (quite the opposite). The Path isn't revealed by channelled Atlantean

Warriors or UFOnauts or visions of the Blessed Virgin Mary. Enlightened beings don't perform miracles or intervene on behalf of this or the other organization-- even Jesus himself didn't perform miracles for people who asked for them. Most mystical traditions state that getting in touch with your past lives or performing magic tricks are actually substantial distractions from the path. Zen monks tell you to ignore visions and prophecies you receive when meditating because they're not the goal. Zen monks don't do card tricks.

Another popular trope, which is really silly when you start to think about it, is that "gnosis is different for everybody." That's a little like saying "objectivity is different for everybody." Consider: stick your hand in a bucket of water, a bowl full of ice, or above a steaming bathtub. What happens? Your hand gets wet. Same kind of deal with gnosis: it may *manifest* differently for everyone, but it doesn't mean anything anyone wants it to. It's specific to certain contexts.

Of course, there is the matter of grace. Grace is the exception to these conditions. The Logos and Sophia can do whatever they want; they may activate the gnosis of the Pleroma at any time, at any moment, in any person. The ways of the Christos and Sophia can't ever truly be known by humans; otherwise, the Archons might learn of their plans and work against them. Their activities in the World of Forms, and those whom they touch, must remain transparent to the Authorities.

So: how do we get this gnosis? Well, if you're interested in gnosis within the limitations of the Black Iron Prison, the person of Knowledge (that's you) can cultivate the gnosis of the Fullness through the Mysteries established by the Christos and Sophia: Devotion to Reason and Living Information, The Ascent Through The Spheres, Mindful Incorporation Into the Continuum of Being.

Devotion to the Word is sincere and honest study of the Living Information as revealed by certain enlightened teachers and their students. The Ascent Through The Spheres is the denial of the Archons and the overcoming of Fate. Mindful Incorporation Into the Continuum of Being is the spiritual methodology of the Buddha.

Having gnosis ain't all fun and games: getting into this stuff means painting a big ol' target on your back with a sign that says, "Come an' get me, Archons!" It also means being incredibly unpopular with a lot of people.

Gnosis isn't merely something that's limited to church or personal ritual. It's not something that's done in soup kitchens or prison ministries. Gnosis is something that happens within each individual Gnostic, every second of every day. Gnosis might drop in on someone during Mass or meditation, but it has no limits; it's just as likely to drop in when you're watching an episode of *Louis* or driving home from work.

And when you have it, you have to try to live it; there is no alternative, nor is there escape. Gnosis expands within you as an awareness, an intimate awareness of a far more subtle understanding or comprehension of the universe. It then becomes a compulsion. If you aren't compelled to live it, you haven't experienced it-- this is an absolute.

Gnosis floods your existence. It saturates you and sits on your shoulders like wet wool. It charges you to do something about it, even if there's nothing you can do. So, you have to try to Live it, as best as you can. You don't have to go to church or take communion, though you can if that's how you're moved. You don't have to say your prayers every night, though that's a good practice. You don't have to meditate every day or even to be nice to other people. You can Live Gnosis by getting up and going to work in the morning. You can live it by writing about it, or by studying it in school. You can live it by forgiving someone who's done you wrong. You can live it by drawing or painting or making music.

All of these things can also **not** be living gnosis. It's up to you. Because, **All that it takes to Live gnosis—to Think Like a Gnostic-- is to allow your gnosis to manifest itself in your interactions with the World**. In computer terms, you have to allow your gnosis to become your input/output device. Everything that comes in gets processed by gnosis. Everything that goes out leaves by gnosis. In that way, you have the opportunity to "live gnosis" every time you talk to anyone whatsoever. You have the opportunity to "live gnosis" when you're deciding what to have on your pizza. You have the opportunity to "live gnosis" when you're playing with your dog, or talking with your friends. A little gnosis might happen in church (in *any* church), but unless you live in your church, eat in your church, sleep and work and interact with other people in your church, most of your gnosis will happen outside of it. In fact, if the only place you're able to contextualize gnosis is in your church, you are not thinking like a Gnostic.

# 13. Anthropology and the Chain of Attainment.

As containers of the Spiritual Seed, which, when activated by the Christos and Sophia, reveals the inbreaking of the Pleroma into the World of Forms, all humans are intrinsically involved with the redemption of the imperfection. This redemption is necessary inasmuch as the completion of the redemption will allow the Limitless Light to truly Know itself in full knowledge of its emanations. For this reason, the imprisonment must also have occurred, for how can the Limitless Light come to know itself if isn't first ignorant of some part of itself?

In one sense, the redemption has already occurred. It's continually occurring. If, indeed, the Limitless Light is eternal and unchanging, then we can't limit it in the constraints of Time. The concept of Time is a concept of limitations, and as a concept of limitations, Time is ruled over by the Archons and their servitors. Thus, the passage of Time is an illusion maintained within the World of Forms. The process of redemption and of the gnosis of the Great Invisible Spirit has-occurred-is-occurring-will-occur. All that is, that appears of change, is but a single instance, a single firing of a single synapse in the Nous.

Now then, according to a Gnostic understanding, humankind exists as three-in-one: the *hylic*, who has surrendered to the Archon, the *pneumatic*, who has joined with the Christos and Sophia, and the *psychic*, who sometimes surrenders to the Archon, and sometimes joins with the Christos and Sophia. Most of us are in the psychic state, which doesn't mean we can read minds; it means we live in a complex world where sometimes we're really cool and sometimes we behave like jackasses.

Of course, it's a huge mistake to say that these are three different types of human *by nature*. It's a dangerous game to start applying labels to other people and making value judgements based on those labels. Claiming that any other person is stuck in some kind of spiritual state, or is less than perfect, is giving in to the power of Fate. And we all know who controls Fate, right? *That's right: the SPACE NAZIS!* (ha ha obviously not really, but claiming that "so-and-so is hylic and not as good as so-and-so who is pneumatic" is just as dangerous as claiming that "so-and-so is Jewish and not as good as so-and-so who is German," to get all Godwin-y on you).

So, we use these aspects as tools for self-understanding, because they're three aspects of **all** humans, all of whom contain the spiritual seed. The Christos and Sophia can awaken gnosis in any one of these aspects; therefore, your best bet is to treat everybody as though they may already be awakened. You can never know where the Christos and Sophia will do their work, because if it's that easy for us, then it's just as easy for the Archons, who could seek the person out, and put that person to death.

Obviously, we find out all the time that a lot of folks who claim to be ascended spiritual masters, and who volunteer in soup kitchens and give money away and such, are scam artists and manipulative narcissists. On the other end of the pole, it's possible for someone with complete gnosis to seem like a jerk who insults people and eats lots of fast food. So it's best to give everybody the benefit of the doubt, at least at first.

Now, let's get a little morbid and talk about what happens to us when we die. As Platonic philosophers with a serious Buddhism fix, we're into the concept of metempsychosis, or "reincarnation." Most individuals experience this constant cycle of birth and rebirth, and are subject to what Eastern religion calls karma, cause and effect, action and reaction. In *This Way*, we call it the Chain of Attainment.

According to this interpretation of Sethian Gnostic mythology, the soul resides within this imperfect chain of attainment until saved via the gnosis of the Logos and Sophia. The redeemed soul, after death, transcends the realms of limitation and becomes one with the experience of the Ultimate Freedom of the Limitless Light. Should a soul remain unredeemed within a lifetime, that soul will be unable to escape the chain of attainment and will be reborn accordingly.

We are big fans of Universalism, that every single soul will eventually achieve this redemption– it's just a matter of "Time."

Indeed, according to our understanding of Time, this redemption has already occurred, as the passage of time is an illusion of the imperfect world.

As far as the pre-existence of the soul, we generally believe that incarnated souls are those which haven't yet escaped the imperfect World of Forms, or, in many cases, are experiencing incarnation for the very first time as part of the ongoing process of material creation.

This system works really well for the Demiurge: he can reward or punish as he sees fit, and maintain his control over the World of Forms. He does this via the medium of the Black Iron Prison and its impelled control systems, which discourage the individual from finding gnosis for herself, instead maintaining that deliverance can only be granted by another.

Unlike Eastern religion, however, in which reincarnation occurs in linear time (i.e. rebirth happens in a 'future lifetime'), it's best to keep in mind that linear time is an Archonic illusion. This is why, in Gnostic scripture, the Archons are assigned the days of the week or signs of the Zodiac—

representations of time and space. In reality, as we know from our discussion above, the Limitless Light transcends space and time to such an extent that what we perceive as motion, change and time would by necessity appear as a single unit to the Limitless Light, as it would perceive every instant simultaneously. If this is the case, then the soul and the accompanying portion of the Limitless Light might be reborn in any "time" and as any individual. You may be reborn as someone living in the time of Jesus, I may be reborn as someone living in the future.

Remember, the Limitless Light is differentiating itself until it has experienced all of the potentialities that it contains. This means that the process of metempsychosis allows the Limitless Light to experience each of its aspects as a single consciousness. There is only one consciousness—it's the one you are experiencing right now, as you read this. It's also the consciousness that I'm experiencing right now as I type this. This is the Limitless Light learning about itself, and it literally means that everyone is everyone else. I might be reborn as you, you might be reborn as me. Gnosis is the personal realization and experience of this fact. *This is a huge secret that I've just let you in on.*

Obviously, not everyone experiences gnosis. Thankfully, Sophia and the Logos are correcting the divine equation by way of iteration. To return to the Chaos Theory analogy, if we're all rounded variables in a fake ordered set which is dictated by an underlying fractal, the Limitless Light and its Aeons are stripping off the "rounding" and returning us to our original natures that exist on the left side of the decimal point.

This is why ritual can be important, and can also be applied to the concept of the eucharist, whereby the Phildickian "plasmates" (living information) are introduced to an iterated formula: ritual that is repeated at regular intervals. This isn't to say that any specific ritual is "right" or "wrong," but rather that Divinity tends to introduce itself into the equation of the World of Forms via iteration.

Back to the idea of the three states of humanity– again, this is all as 'literal' as it needs to be to you. Is it hypostatic, or psychological? Which helps you the most? So. If you die in the state of a hylic aspect, you've been weighed down by the material, and ensnared by the Archon, and will descend back into a body in the World of Forms according to the control system of the Archons. This isn't always a bad thing; it does, however, mean rebirth into the realms of limitations and not into the Pleroma.

If you die in a pneumatic state, you're reborn into the Fullness of the Pleroma as soon as the gnosis is realized. After the death of the body, you ascend into the realms of Perfection, the Fullness, escaping the bonds of the Black Iron Prison and the cycle of incarnation. According to This Way, that spirit, that wonderful and perfected spark of the divine Light, may also become a Messenger of the Light-- a Bodhisattva, taking on a body in the World of Forms out of compassion and mercy for those still trapped within the Prison, along with the Christos and Sophia assisting them with their own resurrections.

Got to repeat it: you can't say for sure what state somebody else was in when they died. This is advice for your own self-discovery, not to be used to judge what happened to other people.

# 14. So what?

Maybe so nothing-- maybe who cares? It's possible you read this book and think, "golly, this is a whole bunch of crazy hoodoo nonsense. Why did I even waste my time?" In that case, the answer to "So what"? is "Yeah, so what?" If it's not for you, it's not for you. No harm, no foul. I'm not here to change any minds, just to get some ideas off of my chest and maybe sell a few books so I can afford to pay for gas.

But if you dig on a Gnostic worldview, it's worth thinking about ways to incorporate it into your daily existence. So, if we go over all of this information, can we drill down to some basic assumptions that directly impact how it can help us interact with the world?

For me, the following dataset sums up my place in the World, and informs my Worldview:

- **One:** **Existence is Imperfection.**
- **Two: The** origin of **imperfection is separation**

from the Fullness of the Pleroma.

- **Three: It's possible to reconnect to the Pleroma.**
- **Four: Reconnection to the Pleroma is possible via the cultivation of gnosis.**

Perfection is an impossibility in the World of Forms. Existence is predicated on a confluence of Living Information, both valid and invalid, that we're unable to properly process without special preconditions having been met. We get here, we become subject to a whole series of impelled systems over which we have no control, from the dress code at work to the laws of physics. We can spend all of our time working on understanding these systems, but invariably, our attempts to do so will be thwarted.

Since we're products of an imperfect world, it's never safe to trust any information you're given by any source ever that you can't somehow verify. This means you constantly need to ask questions no matter what. It's super important to be skeptical, critical and distrustful of everything originating from any human system. Once you feel like you've really uncovered the truth behind something, KEEP DIGGING and find out what's really underneath, because whatever is on the surface becomes some degree of false as soon as it's observed. This doesn't mean you have to rebel against everything; sometimes you might question something and find out it's okay. What it **does** mean is that you have to **test everything against Reason**.

It also may be most satisfying to operate under the assumption that if you're not directly in control of a situation, the "worst" possible outcome is the most likely. Now, the Universe contains far too many factors to know any outcome with certainty, and good things definitely happen, but the less you are engaged in a situation, the greater likelihood that you won't be keen on the results.

Why'd things go so far South? It's because Wisdom (Sophia) went too far without Reason (Logos). You can be totally wise, but when you're unreasonable, too, things aren't going to work out for you, and vice-versa.

There are all of these perfect qualities–valid information– out there that we strive towards (the Aeons), but given that we're in a limited, imperfect place, governed by time and fate, we can't get to them. We're sitting inside an enormous fractal that's patterned on the Pleroma, which means there are patterns upon patterns. It's possible to learn to read these patterns and recognize historical iterations, if you're so inclined, but you also have to expect a lot of flotsam and jetsam. You also have to expect meddling from Archonic forces, be they psychological or hypostatic.

Separation from the Pleroma caused that bad information we're talking about. But, you can learn to spot bad information, and to look for it in everything. You can also learn to filter it out, like tuning a radio dial, so you can start picking up the good stuff. When you start messing with your tuner, though, it's a good bet that something out there will start picking up on you.

It's good to have a plan, and your plan might be hanging out with your friends and family, having a good time, playing music or games or watching TV, or maybe gardening. Any of these things are perfectly fine ways to reconnect with the Pleroma. As I've said before, this Way isn't for people who are happy and contented and already have a sense of purpose. Or, maybe, you're like me, and it helps to have a toolkit– some technologies and semiotics that help make that connection.

Either way, and whatever you decide, now you have a better idea of what it means to Think Like a Gnostic.

# Part Two: A Gnostic Worldview in Practice

# The Universe is Gaslighting You

*"If I were not mad, I could have helped you. Whatever you had done, I could have pitied and protected you. But because I am mad, I hate you. Because I am mad, I have betrayed you. And because I'm mad, I'm rejoicing in my heart, without a shred of pity, without a shred of regret, watching you go with glory in my heart!"* Paula Anton, *"Gaslight"*

Paranoid much?

No, really-- ever have the feeling that the Universe is out to get you? Ever consider that maybe that's because it's?

They're out to get you. Oh, I'm not talking about facile and overcomplicated conspiracy theories, like chemtrails or the New World Order or anti-vaccination silliness or 9/11 Truthers or Zionist plots or whatever; those issues are all moot, and red herrings. They're beside the point, and may contain their own different levels of "truthiness," but they're mere facets of the major systems behind the fabric of our shared reality. What I'm talking about is the irrational nature of the Kosmos itself, the darkly buzzing feedback inherent to the World of Forms, which is governed by the Archons, the very talons of Fate and all of its essential annoyances.

This feedback, you see, is designed to make you doubt your own reality. Just as the murderous husband in the old movie enacted his nefarious plan to make his wife think she was crazy, so the Demiurge and his Archonic henchmen are flickering the lights in your house. They're stomping around upstairs when you're sure you're all alone. They're stealing your stuff and hiding it in strange places. They're making you stub your toe, and clogging your gutters, and micromanaging your time at work.

What I mean is that it's not the Big Stuff that proves the Universe is insane, it's the little stuff. The Big Stuff is abstract to most of us; those of us who do get exposed to the Big Stuff know for a fact that this place is nuts. War, poverty, disaster; get touched by one of these, and you don't need convincing. The little stuff, though... even the person who thinks her life is perfect, who has everything she needs, everything she desires, even that person has to go to the dentist, gets stuck in traffic, catches a cold. This is the imperfection of existence, the separation from the Fullness that's gaslighting us, making us think that we're the problem, when the Kosmos itself is just as much at fault. The Prince of this World is, after all, his King Daddy's Little Boy.

But, there's Good News! You're not insane![14]

Getting irritated by small things? It's not because you have a bad attitude. It's because you're *normal.* Tired of the day-to-day grind, and feel as though you're being put through your paces by a nonsensical system designed to malfunction as often as possible in the smallest, most infuriating way? *That's a healthy point of view.* Sick of the hippy-dippy platitudes of rich jerks who think you can wish yourself into perfection? *Don't let the*

---

[14] Well, you might be, from a medical standpoint, but this is a metaphor, get me?

*Kosmos trick you into thinking you can't be fed up.*

See, just like Paula figures out in the movie, once you know their tricks, and realize that hey, you're the sane one here, then you're On Top. It doesn't, of course, mean you get to be an obnoxious jerk, or that you can stop putting up with their nonsense. Your toe will still hurt when you kick something hard. You'll still catch that cold, and your computer will still crash at the most inopportune moment. You can't escape that, not while you're still living in this World of Forms.

However, it does mean that you can be comfortably skeptical. You can realize that it's all a bunch of tricks, and you can get out from underneath that Kenomic Worldview and start recognizing the illusion. You can start to recognize that there is a lot of total bullshit out there, and you don't have to feel bad or guilty or wrong for calling it out as bullshit.

That's GNOSIS, people, and it can be yours for FREE!

# Don't Compare Yourself With Others

> *"Keep silence and don't compare yourself with others." – Abba Bessarion*

————————-

One of the worst things you can do is compare yourself with other people– that's one way the archons can really get you! It's very easy to do, but it's almost always a bad idea; you're the one your self-image impacts, so what do those people matter?

One of the most obvious and pernicious examples is body image. The damnable archons of Popular Culture will always parade the latest idiocy that they'd like to see you emulate. Currently, it's too-skinny, but consider that this may actually be an improvement over the days of wasp-waists and children's girdles:

If heavier ever becomes fashionable, look for fat-suit catalogues and "skinny-shaming." Really, where body-image is concerned, the only two questions you should ask yourself are 1) Am I relatively healthy? (i.e. not anorexic or morbidly obese) and 2) Am I satisfied with my own damn body? Any other questions are pointless, and it's nobody else's concern.

But this is, of course, all cliché by now. At least, people **say** it's cliché, even though we all know it's still a huge problem. It takes lots of self-reflection and anti-brainwashing to get people to realize that comparing their physical looks to other peoples' is a fool's game.

The tendency to compare ourselves to others takes far more insidious shape, however, in the little things we do every day. For example, suppose you're driving your car, and you're stuck in a line trying to get off of the freeway after work (I'm looking at you, I-5 exit to the West Seattle Bridge). A conscientious driver, you merged into the exit lane back when traffic was moving at a fair pace, but right before you get to the exit ramp, some jackass in a souped-up SUV swerves into the lane a few cars ahead of you from the swiftly moving lane on the left and gets onto the ramp after 30 seconds, when you've been waiting for twenty minutes, dammit! I know what you're thinking, because it's probably what I'm thinking when that happens to me: THAT ISN'T FAIR! I would totally never do that! There are unwritten rules of the road, and if we were all a little more thoughtful drivers, and maybe I should (have a stern chat with him/follow him home/pull up alongside him and shoot him/etc. etc. etc.).

The underlying problem? **I'm comparing myself to that dude, and getting all worked up about it.** There is no fairness in the World of Forms, there is simply That Which Happens. It's okay to get annoyed about it– *in fact, it's perfectly normal.* But if you react by thinking, "He got in ahead of me, and I am a nicer driver than he's because I merged when it was convenient for other people," then you're reacting by comparing yourself to him, and he's in your brain like a crazy brain parasite. Listen, you've only got enough room in your brain for a few crazy brain parasites before your head explodes, and it's all because the root of your issue with this guy is that "he's a jerk, and by comparison, you a better."

This is, of course, not to say that you can't call a jackass a jackass, just that you shouldn't go around comparing yourself to jackasses. Man, we do that a lot!

Every time we think about how awesome it would be to be that rich guy, or that famous guy, or to have that sweet house the dude down the street has, you're comparing yourself to that person, but the only result is to underline what you consider your own negative qualities. Your self-comparisons to that guy aren't going to make you rich or famous or house-ier, and whether you think you're better than someone won't change their behavior one bit.

It's a trickier proposition when it comes to people you look up to, but when you really start to look at it, it's just as dangerous to compare yourself to people who are, even objectively, great. To begin, even people who seem objectively great aren't always what you think they are. Let's take ol' M.K. Gandhi, for example; it's difficult to find somebody whose impact on history and general 'goodness' are more agreed-upon... which is why it's all the more jarring to find out he was abusive to his wife, and into some weird, weird sex. This begs the question: when you have a role model, what "role" are you emulating? If you compare yourself to Gandhi, is it the Gandhi who helped liberate India, or the Gandhi who came up with creepy "experiments" that included sleeping with the wives of his ashram members and his own naked niece (problematic whether literal or figurative)?

If there is one idea we should really banish from our society for perpetuating even worse ideas, it's the idea of the "role model." When one has a role model, one can only end up disappointed in their shortcomings, or disappointed in one's own inability to live up to the high standards we wish to emulate. Does the comparison even have merit? What good is it to compare one's self to Gandhi when one isn't involved in liberating a country? Worse yet, what if the person you're emulating is a complete asshole, like the characters in Ayn Rand's trashy novels? And, what if that person is a complete asshole, but you don't even know it? How many ex-Scientologists wish they hadn't gone around comparing themselves to senior members, or to ol' L. Ron Hubbard himself?

Nope, it's better to make your decision based on your experiences instead of comparing yourself to other people. Not that these kind of comparisons are really even possible, of course– each one of us is an aggregate of countless influences and indications and qualities, and to truly compare yourself to someone else, to say with certainty that "My X is like/unlike Your Y," one would need to take all of these factors into account. So, when you're comparing yourself to someone else, you're really only comparing yourself to your false image of that person, and when that happens, you're starting to tickle the fancy of the archons!

Racism and bigotry are obvious examples of thought-patterns in people who compare themselves to false images, and make judgments based on these fake constructs. But, what about my traffic example above? Or the body image issue? Or, even the Gandhi issue? Can you see how these also involve the practice of creating images that don't match up with reality? Do you really want to base your actions, thoughts, goals or ideas based on a falsehood that exists only in your mind? Because the archons really love that, let me tell you what.

So, what do you do? How do you keep from comparing yourself to a child's drawing you've created in your head of qualities you think somebody has? Ol' Bessarion told us one possible answer: keep silence. This is especially helpful if you find yourself comparing yourself to some jerk because you feel like something's not fair, like our traffic example above. Once you've let off your steam (because you will need to let off steam and that's okay), shut the hell up for a minute and don't think about anything. This is a lot easier to do if you're used to inner silence; meditating and praying are always helpful in this regard. Then reflect, silently, that comparing yourself to that person is a waste of time and energy. What's done is done, and in the grinding feedback of the World of Forms, you can't expect "fairness" from the Kosmos.

So, be silent. The constant noise and buzzing of the archons hates silence.

Another thing you could do, if you like somebody and find yourself starting to draw comparisons, is to separate the qualities from the person. I don't want to compare myself to Gandhi, but I can be inspired by his compassion for others. I don't want to compare myself to the bastard who cuts me off on the road, but I can strive not to cut off other people. As I raise my son, I hope to inspire him to emulate what may be my better qualities. On the other hand, if I'm ever a jerk, I don't want him to do what I'm doing. I don't want to be my son's role model-- I want him to learn to appreciate positive qualities wherever they may occur, and to recognize that even the people he looks up to the most aren't always worth comparison to one's own experience. After all, how many bastards are bastards because their fathers were bastards, and their fathers before them, etc.?

This is definitely one of those behaviors that you can't escape while you're down here in the World of Forms-- it's an innate quality in humankind. However, one of the things that divides us from the animals is our ability to (attempt to) overcome our innate qualities. Although we'll almost certainly never perfect the ability to stop comparing ourselves to other people, we can definitely give it the old Gnostic try.

# Archons, Meet the Archons

**Seven In One Blow!**

(To the tune of "Meet the Flintstones")

Archons, meet the Archons,
They're a pathway to insanity.

From the Outer Darkness,
But they're still a lot like you and me.

Let's ride underneath the mercy seat.
In the Demiurge's bucket seat.

When you're with the Archons
you'll have a roller coaster ride time.

A deep inside time.
You'll have a nightmare time!

Ladies and gentlemen, let's bring out our special guests! Here they are, your beloved rulers, LIVE and in PERSON! Here are their fashion secrets, their relationship advice, their money-making tips and MORE! Without further ado, we are proud to introduce, for their first-ever appearance here in your town, the ARCHONS!

## Athoth

**Current Residence:** The Moon
**Interests:** Goodness, Psychology, Magic, Feminism, Tides
**Head of:** A Sheep
**Favorite Song:** "Sheep," The Housemartins
**Favorite Food:** Guatemalan Insanity Pepper
**Favorite Book:** *The Interpretation of Dreams* by Sigmund Freud
**Favorite Demiurge:** "Yaldabaoth, of course!"
**People Would Be Surprised To Know:** "I enjoy forcing people to do good things. It's fun, and good for the delicious, delicious soul!"

# Eloaios

**Current Residence:** Mercury

**Interests:** Providence, Thriftiness, Business Transactions, Communications

**Head of:** A Donkey

**Favorite Song:** "Taking Care of Business," Bachmann Turner Overdrive

**Favorite Food:** Hay

**Favorite Book:** *Who Moved My Cheese* by Spencer Johnson

**Favorite Demiurge:** "Big ol' shout-out to my main man Yaldabaoth!"

**People Would Be Surprised To Know:** "I work quite frequently as a political consultant for the Democratic Party."

# Astaphaios

**Current Residence:** Venus
**Interests:** Love, Lust, Desire, Divinity, Consumption
**Head of:** A Hyena
**Favorite Song:** "I'm Gonna Make You Love Me," Diana Ross, the Supremes, the Temptations
**Favorite Food:** "Whatever you're having"
**Favorite Book:** Eat, Pray, Love by Elizabeth Gilbert
**Favorite Demiurge:** "That's a tricky one, but my heart will always belong to Yaldabaoth."
**People Would Be Surprised To Know:** "The way to my heart is definitely through my stomach."

# Yao

**Current Residence:** the Sun

**Interests:** Self-gratification, Myself, the Arts, Music

**Head of:** A Seven Headed Snake

**Favorite Song:** "Take Me Out to the Ballgame," Trad.

**Favorite Food:** "Anything from Bobby Flay."

**Favorite Book:** Song of Myself by Walt Whitman

**Favorite Demiurge:** "Yaldabaoth is Number One! You might say I'm his 'Mini-me.'"

**People Would Be Surprised To Know:** "No surprises– I am pretty much awesome."

# Sabaoth

**Current Residence:** Mars

**Interests:** Strategy, Defense, War, Sports

**Head of:** A Dragon

**Favorite Song:** "Momma Said Knock You Out," LL Cool Jay

**Favorite Food:** War Cakes

**Favorite Book:** Starship Troopers by Robert Heinlein

**Favorite Demiurge:** "Yaldabaoth is Mon General."

**People Would Be Surprised To Know:** "I'm really a big softie. Why, just the other day I let a guy keep a thumb and one finger so he could still hold his pencil and write his confession himself."

# Adonin

**Current Residence:** Jupiter
**Interests:** Politics
**Head of:** A Monkey
**Favorite Song:** "This Land Is Your Land," Woodie Guthrie
**Favorite Food:** Freedom Fries
**Favorite Book:** Atlas Shrugged by Ayn Rand
**Favorite Demiurge:** "Vote for Yaldabaoth, every time.'"
**People Would Be Surprised To Know:** "I don't have any party affiliation."

# Sabbataios

**Current Residence:** Saturn

**Interests:** Agriculture, Civilization, Structure, Career

**Head of:** Flame and Fire

**Favorite Song:** "Light My Fire," The Doors

**Favorite Food:** Anything barbecued well-done, especially my own children

**Favorite Book:** *Poor Richard's Almanack* by Ben Franklin

**Favorite Demiurge:** "Yaldabaoth gets things done.'"

**People Would Be Surprised To Know**: "I'm not fat, just big-tentacled."

# What Good is Your Philosophy?

Is your philosophy any good? I mean that in the most literal sense. A lot of people think that a philosophy (be it religious or secular) is something you just *have*. Maybe it's something you're born with, or maybe it's something you decided you like, so you *have* it, and there you are. "I am a Stoic. I believe in Stoicism." "I am a Christian. I believe in Christianity." "I am a Buddhist. I believe in Buddhism."

But listen, that's no good. You can't just "have" a philosophy. If your philosophy is going to do you any good whatsoever, you have to *live* it.

What does that mean, *living* a philosophy? It certainly doesn't mean going to church, or praying, or meditating; although these things can be components of living a philosophy, they're obvious. What it means is living a Way of some kind that impacts the moments *between* these kind of events. It's all well and good to have a philosophy that calls for regular meditation, and to then spend an hour every other day meditating. All that philosophy is really doing, though, is influencing the time you're spending meditating. That's kind of pointless.

The same with church, or prayer. If all your philosophy gives you is what you get out of church, or prayer, or ritual or whatever, then you're doing it wrong. That stuff-- the sacraments, the rituals, the rites-- that's all fluff (unless, of course you're a priest or something). Sure, it's good to do if that's your bag, but if your philosophy is only good for occasional special moments, why even bother? What you need to take from your philosophy is a reason for, and a reaction to, your every day existence.

A good philosophy should be a constant background noise, an ambiance that one can detect behind everything you do and say. A good philosophy is just as present when you're driving to work or watching a movie as it's at church. It's just as present when you're shopping for clothes or riding the bus as it's during meditation. It gives you a reason for most things that happen to you, and gives you a reaction to them, as well.

A lot of people make a lot of money on the idea that a good philosophy needs to make you happy, or get you stuff. This is definitely not necessarily the case; in point-of-fact, many good philosophies produce a sincere disquietude in those who live them. This is one of the interesting facets of the Gnostic philosophy, for instance, as I describe it in *This Way*:

> The earmark of the Pleromic individual isn't happiness, but dignity and confidence. You may be depressed and miserable with your circumstances in the World of Forms, but underneath you understand and know that the Good exists, that the Present is temporary and eternal, and– more importantly– what these things mean and how they effect your lifestyle. You carry yourself with a healthy posture, respectful of, and interested in, the experiences you have. The Pleromic Worldview can just as readily manifest as what appears to be foolishness or childishness, but this is rare, and dignity is maintained.

The Gnostic Way works for me, because it gives me a reason for everything that happens (i.e. the default state of the World of Forms is imperfection, the Archons screw stuff up, the proper application of Wisdom and Reason helps deal with the Archons), and gives me a way to react to it (be really skeptical of everything, be nice to other people as much as possible, be bone-shakingly honest about everything). Some days are wretched and stressful and nasty, but if I live this philosophy and make sure it's always on in the background, that's OK.

Now, don't get me wrong– it's entirely possible to live your philosophy to an unhealthy extreme. It's possible, in fact, to let your philosophy live you. Examples are all over the place– people who get so wrapped up in an idea that they're consumed by it, until it cuts off all healthy skepticism and it becomes Archonic and tries to escape. This can happen with religious fundamentalists, but it can also happen with anybody who lets her philosophy take over and start walking around and making loud, uncomfortable sounds.

This is why I describe the best philosophy as background noise that colors everything. A philosophy is most effective when it stays in the background, when it's a polite influence, and doesn't come to the forefront of your interactions with the World of Forms. It's best to maintain your philosophy as a kind of white noise. If you let your philosophy live you, instead of vice-versa, that's when things can get icky.

In short: don't be satisfied with a philosophy that you stick in your back pocket or wear around your neck to show off. Make sure your philosophy is a Good one, one you can use all the time. Don't let it get out of hand, or only use it on occasion; instead, cultivate it during the small, otherwise insignificant times. Then you'll be living it, which is pretty neat.

# Know Traffic, Know Yourselves

I bring up traffic fairly frequently– it's a fantastic shared experience we can use to discuss our interaction with the World of Forms. In fact, I have a theory that 3/5 of the problems we have interacting with one another on a day-to-day basis are caused by traffic. Not, mind you, traffic that moves too fast; I'm not discussing fatalities, which have actually dropped in recent years[15] because it's becoming increasingly expensive to fill gas tanks. I'm talking about traffic that moves too slowly.[16]

(Although, as an early aside, I often think that a better choice for assassination if one had the ubiquitous "rhetorical time machine" would be Henry Ford. Not only could one then perhaps mitigate the dreadful violence caused by the personal automobile, one would also remove Hitler's greatest Anti-

---

[15]http://www.latimes.com/news/nation/nationnow/la-na-nn-traffic-deaths-20120507,0,3663215.story

[16]http://www.foreignpolicy.com/articles/2010/08/24/the_world_s_worst_traffic?page=0,0

Semitic influence.[17] Of course, this is the World of Forms we're talking about; both genocide and commuting were inevitabilities from the get-go.)

Back to my theory: those of us who do commute in an urban environment are often involved in a daily slog, tellingly described in one of the links above as "soul-crushing." As an example, my personal drive to work takes fifteen minutes during off-hours, but during busy traffic times, can take as much as a complete hour. **That this is considered a 'normal' situation is patently insane.**

When we sit in this traffic, inching forward, we suffer both internal and external indignities. Externally, we have to put up with the dreaded Other Driver-- the jerks who own the road, who feel the need to 'win' at the commute, who impede the flow of traffic, who are willing to risk other peoples' lives to arrive ten seconds sooner. Regardless of the reason for these attitudes in Other Drivers, of course, they're always Someone Else, never You.

Meanwhile, the internal indignity takes place within the confines of the vehicle.

---

[17] http://en.wikipedia.org/wiki/The_International_Jew

Enclosed in an automobile, the driver can only reasonably manifest her reaction to the Other Driver via ineffective outbursts or signals or hand gestures (which, of course, transform her into an Other Driver). There are unreasonable ways to manifest reaction, of course-- road rage, etc.-- but we're talking about the average person, not the person likely to snap and start shooting.

There is another, often overlooked effect of the traffic jam on the individual, which is that most people aren't used to long periods of self-reflection. The combination of the frustration of being kept from one's goal, especially during the evening commute when one is returning to one's home, and the unusual circumstance, for most people, of having "nothing to do" leads to a level of introspection that all too often causes one to meditate on frustration.

We seem to think that boiling over in a vehicle for two hours every day, impotently speculating on the Other Driver and the frustrations of unmet anticipations is something happening in a vacuum, that once our destination is reached and we exit the vehicle, everything that has happened while driving vanishes. In reality, however, this introspection on frustration can't help but boil over into the day-to-day interactions one has with other people.

Think about the situation outside of the context of the vehicle: Say you're confined in a tiny room without much to do. You can't even leave your chair. You have no idea when you'll be able to exit the room-- will it be after fifteen minutes, or an hour? Outside, you can see people blatantly putting other peoples' lives at risk, including your own. You can yell and scream at them, or flick them off, but there is literally no way anything you say or do will influence them, even if they were able to hear you. You expect when you finally leave the room, you'll leave it free of consequence? Now imagine you have to do it every day. **Twice**.

In actuality, we *must* carry with us whatever happens in the car throughout the day. The perception that the frustrations of the commute end with the commute means these frustrations are often suppressed, and it's very likely that they'll manifest in other ways. Since we can't take out these frustrations on the ones who caused the problem– the Other Drivers–and since we can't properly process our meditations on frustration, we take them out on those around us.

Sure, we usually hold it in just fine. Those of us lucky enough to have outlets for our general frustrations–– meditation, maybe therapy, killing zombies on a console–– may be able to simply batch these feelings with all the rest and deal with them. But, although there's no way to provide empirical proof, my theory is that otherwise collected individuals, after being subjected to this level of inability to express frustration day after day after day, express it in other ways, and that these manifestations of frustration, which seem otherwise irrational, drive (pardon the pun) a great deal of negative social interaction.

Maybe you don't drive; maybe you're the passenger, or you take the bus, which is also engaged in the consequences of the traffic jam. In that case, you're still subject to the consequences of this situation on the driver. And, regardless of whether we get stuck in traffic in any capacity, we're all on the receiving end of this displaced frustration broadcast by those who do drive every day.

Even if you take the bullet-train and have a lovely, productive commute, you likely work, or live with, or live around people who are subject to this phenomenon.

**This, my friends, is the Archons in action.** The Archons are most insidious when we encounter them in day-to-day existence; it isn't politics or conspiracy theories where we're most likely to encounter them, but in the small daily situations over which we have no control. Or, at least, it *seems* like we have no control. They're the causes, the tiny butterflies (in this case, the frustrations I've detailed) that cause the hurricanes that can destroy us. Yes, if you're stuck in traffic, you can blame the Archons for your situation.

So what do we do? Some would suggest we just stop driving, but that's utterly naive, especially for the average working person. Without an Earth-shattering change of some kind, the option to simply stop driving is pretty impractical for most people at this point, in this economy, where you'd better darned well be able to get to work and public transportation isn't well-funded. Maybe we'll luck out, and the cities will finally transition away from the auto-centric model, and we'll all live close enough to work to walk, and there'll be nice bike-lanes and no hills, or we can telecommute, or use public transportation. *And then maybe everyone gets a free puppy that doesn't poop and never loses its puppy fur.*

The way I see it, there are two levels that need to be addressed to help at least mitigate some of this traffic-related exasperation. The first level concerns the frustration with the Other Driver, and there are a few things we can do to make interacting with other drivers a little easier.

**Accept that you will be cut off, that jerks are out there who are asshole drivers.** This is difficult to do, but you can do it. It works best if you imagine that all of these jerks have good reasons for their jerky behavior. Maybe that dude who cut you off is trying to get to the hospital where his wife is giving birth to a baby. Maybe that idiot putting on her makeup is a single mom who didn't have time to do it at home, but desperately needs to get to an important job interview so she can feed her kids. I know, chances are it's self-centered turkeys who don't care one whit about other people, but at least some of them have to have a good reason, so why not give them the benefit of the doubt?

Traffic becomes impeded and slows down when someone is trying to change lanes but can't. So, no matter the situation, even if it's someone unfairly cutting into a lane or cutting you off, **if someone wants to get in front of you, let them.** Period. Don't be a dick and speed up and keep them from getting in front of you, because if you do that, you're frustrating **everyone behind the person who is trying to change lanes but can't.** It's easier, and nicer, to just let up on the gas, be courteous, and let them in. *There is **never** a good reason not to let someone in front of you.*

Traffic also becomes impeded and slows down when cars get too close to one another. Then you end up with tailgaters and rear-enders and slower traffic and it's just an unending circle of frustration. Not only that, but one of the biggest causes of "phantom" traffic jams -- gridlock with no apparent instigator-- is... tailgating! The solution? **Don't freakin' tailgate.** If you are a driver, **you should always be able to see the**

**back tires of the car in front of you.** If someone is tailgating you, **immediately let them pass if you can.**

Finally, if someone does something that annoys you, **scream.** Curse, yell or shout, or sing really loud. Why not? Screw those guys. Let it out in the car, don't carry it with you when you leave.

The second level concerns the forced introspection you're stuck with when you're driving. To help with this, we recommend the following:

**Don't drive alone, if being bored annoys you.** Drive with a friend, or loved one, or carpool, and come up with fun games you can play, or things you can talk about. Whenever my wife and I have the opportunity to drive in together, we always discuss "what's on tap for the day," and use the time as an extra chance to catch up. Don't text and drive, though– that's just ridiculous.

Have to drive alone? **Listen to something that you like.** Make it a point to listen to the radio or an interesting audiobook.

Conversely, don't listen to anything whatsoever, but **use the drive as an**

**opportunity for mindfulness**. Why not use the time to meditate?

Also, you should really try to **drive for fun** every now and again. Go on a pleasant Sunday drive with the fam, find an empty stretch of road and go really fast, build good associations with being in the car.

As always, these are ways for **you** to deal with the frustrations of driving, but really encourage other people to be conscientious drivers, too. Every time we get in the car, we're doing something incredibly dangerous with a bunch of strangers. Shouldn't we want to ask them to be careful?

Now for the Secret Part: this whole discussion is a metaphor for existence, if you really think about it. The car is the body, the road is the World of Forms with its arbitrary rules, all established by the Archons. My question for you is, in this scenario, who are the Aeons? What is the element of gnosis? How will your commute home tonight be different than it was this morning? There are right and wrong answers....

# Why Marriage Equality is Worth It: A Gnostic Perspective

One of the arguments you hear a lot regarding marriage equality is the "bigger fish to fry" argument. You actually hear it quite a bit from fairly reasonable people: "there are so many horrible things going on right now. Can't we just put the whole gay marriage thing aside and focus on stuff that's really important?" It does make a kind of sense; the homosexual population is a very small minority, so why is so much energy being spent on an issue that affects so few, when we could be focusing on war and health care and whatnot, and take care of the marriage 'debate' later (as though such a thing could be debated) .

A Gnostic friend of mine exemplified this argument with a comment on Facebook the other day:

> Rome is burning, and gays and straights will share the same pyre while

the emperors play their satanic fiddles. Distraction is one of the great tools of the Archons.

He's right about one thing: distraction **is** one of the great tools of the Archons. I posit, however, that my friend has his distractions mixed-up, that the true distractions are the big-picture power plays of politics and celebrity, and the thing they're distracting us from is *taking care of one another*.

I realized some time ago that Big Politics with its symbolism, conspiracies, shadowy cabals, etc.-- all of this information is amazing, but what is its real-life application for the average reader? This material falls on the spectrum between "Outlandish/possibly spurious" and "Holy crap, my worst fears are confirmed," but it doesn't often happen that "This is applicable to my day-to-day routine" falls anywhere on that spectrum.

What I eventually realized is that if, indeed, 'conspiracies' exist (and I still maintain that the most powerful conspiracy is the confederacy between power, money and stupidity), and even if the political scene is designed as a control system to keep the lower classes supporting the upper classes, **there's not a whole lot that I can do about it.** The war between the Aeons and the Archons takes place on a larger scale than we can even **begin** to imagine. All I can ever do is speculate about what's going on behind closed doors, whether secret organizations are planning mass genocide Unless I'm somehow recruited by Grant Morrison's Invisibles or end up wealthy or debased enough to join the Outer Church, that's not going to change any time soon.

As a consequence, any time I spend getting worked up about politics, or the influence of corporations in modern food production, or the secret Masonic Symbolism in the Denver Airport[18] is time I could be spending *actually doing something*. Yes, distraction is one of the tools of the Archons, but the Big Picture stuff is the distraction.

The Political Scene, and the conspiracies that go along with it, are simply additional forms of celebrity entertainment,

---

[18]  This is really a thing! See http://skeptoid.com/episodes/4194.

and our influence over what happens in a boardroom somewhere in the secret underground base of the Nine Rulers of the World is absolutely negligible. There is no difference between a political debate and American Idol; under the surface, they're both intended to keep you from doing something nice for someone by making you feel you're contributing to a system that requires essentially no participation. **The Big Evil is the distraction; it's keeping us from cultivating the Little Good.**

So what can I actually do, then? I can spend that time doing something useful, like growing my own food. I can head out to my back yard and toss the ball for my dog, which he loves. I can read *Frog and Toad are Friends* to my son. And *I can be concerned that some of my friends aren't legally allowed to get married in most of the country.*

I mean, this is a no-brainer; the fact that gays are a small minority means **it's even *more important* that they have the same rights as everyone else.** Why? Because the Archons know that one of the best ways we can defeat them is through kindness to one another *on the most basic level*, and compassion for those who have no power *on the most essential level.*

It's tempting to want to change the system from the top down, through politics or war or figuring out who is influencing whom, but the fact is that the system can't be changed that way, it will only be co-opted. Witness the commercialization of environmentalism, or the commodification of the Occupy groups. This is the way in which, to paraphrase Philip Dick, those who fight the Empire are doomed to become the Empire.

Instead, what if we were all to simply practice kindness, to spend what little political influence we have on making it easier for people to be kind to one another? Isn't this part of the idea behind, for example, Dan Savage's "It Gets Better" project[19]– individuals doing small things to make it a little easier for all of us? Top-down change never works; it's only when we have the chance to love one another, and to help others be kind to one another, that we make a real difference.

This isn't to say it's not worth asking the Big Questions, that learning about the Big

---

[19] http://www.itgetsbetter.org

Picture is a total waste of time. The problem comes when we focus on the Big Picture so intently that we lose sight of the small importances in our lives. This is how the Archons get us–– they make it so interesting to watch the massive explosion in the distance that we miss the bee sitting on our arm.

I think it's time for a down-to-earth, practical approach to the Gnostic path, which is why I'm writing about stuff like traffic and marriage equality instead of about how the Archons are behind the Bilderbergs. These are issues we can actually influence, and that should be of tantamount concern in our day-to-day lives. Instead of looking for the Archons that pull the strings up in the clouds, let's take a look for the ones hiding under the bed and the ones keeping people who love one another from getting married.

# Seeing Double: The Counterfeit Spirit, Generalizations and Cause and Effect

One of humanity's tragic flaws is our inability to properly ascertain true causality, which is augmented by our propensity to generalize. Overcoming this problem really requires *beginning to see individuals as individuals*, a task typically difficult at best, but ultimately worth pursuing as part of any path towards understanding.

From a purely Darwinian survivalist standpoint, generalizing is extremely helpful. After all, making the intellectual leap from "This Sabre-toothed tiger is dangerous" to "All Sabre-toothed tigers are dangerous," or "this berry killed Ogg" to "these berries kill people" was definitely a good decision. This is an ability found in most successful species (though not all– we wonder about the Dodo's equation of 'this guy with a stick seems nice' to 'all guys with sticks seem nice'). Because it's such an ingrained aspect of having a brain, the propensity to generalize is innate, almost as automatic as respiration.

However, generalization's usefulness ends at exactly the point at which the thought process requires more than the utilization of the lizard brain. It's great for, say, not getting hit by cars (imagine if we had to learn not to be hit by each different model of car), but when it comes to human interaction, that's where we start getting into trouble. When discussing generalization in relation to cause and effect, if we begin using this perceived cause and effect for value judgments, we do things like start wars, initiate pogroms and start political parties, all of which are as detrimental to our continued survival as Ogg's berry.

The problem is that the difference between the individual and the general is often pronounced enough to negate the efficacy of generalization. In these cases, generalizing can actually rob us of experience! If we'd stopped eating all berries after Ogg died, we'd never try strawberries. If we stopped making all music after the first dissonant chord, we'd never have had My

Bloody Valentine[20]. The complexity and absolute imperfection of the World of Forms makes true generalization an impossibility.

This has a dire impact on our understanding of cause and effect. Let's leave aside, for a moment, the difficulties of proving causality, and work from the standpoint that, "If A, Then B" is a valid statement, at least within the World of Forms as we perceive it. Applied to our above statements on generalization, our innate understanding of cause and effect in this regard could be summarized as, "If the individual, then the general (If this berry killed Ogg, all berries will kill Ogg)" or, "If the general, then the individual (If these are the berries that killed Ogg, I shouldn't eat this berry)." Now let's look at a couple of additional examples of this thought process in action:

"If this Muslim killed all of these people, then all Muslims are evil."

"My hard-earned wages shouldn't be used to pay for lazy illegals."

---

[20] The band, of course.

"Why should I have to use my tax dollars to pay for some good-for-nothing's health care?"

You get the idea. Yes, these are incredibly heavy-handed and clichéd examples, but they're indicative of the attitudes of those who fall into the error I'm discussing. But, this begs the question, can this error in understanding be corrected by simply generalizing in the other direction? Absolutely not, and this is the problem with the "Lipstick Liberal" approach, which condemns, on the one hand, discrimination against minorities (generalities) while turning a blind eye to specific egregious instances of abuse or idiocy (vide the whole "Mohammed Cartoon" fiasco). Of course, those who vilify liberals in general for Lipstick Liberals fall back into the same trap, like those who vilify conservatives in general because of the Tea Party.

In this Way, we have an anthroposophical interpretation of this phenomenon which helps us to understand why it happens. Most of my readers are probably familiar with the importance in the Christian tradition of the figure of the "little child." According to our interpretation, when Jesus talks about being "like a little child," he's referring to the accident-less state of Being in which the essential self exists. We can use an infant as a metaphor. No babies are born "evil" or "good." As an infant grows older, it takes on various attributes through its interactions with the World of Forms. These attributes are then projected by the essential self and, while interacting within the world, are the only facets of the essential self that can typically be perceived, by others **and** by the self.

We find an interesting correlate in Buddhist thought that also helps here. According to Buddhist phenomenology, what humans perceive as "selfness" is actually the five skandhas, also known as "five heaps": form (rupa), sensation (vedana), perception (sanna), mental formations (sankhara) and consciousness (vinanna).

Coming to the realization that all of these skandhas are essentially ephemeral and changing is a key facet of Gautama's original teaching found in the Heart Sutra. Confusing one's "Self" with any one of the skandhas, or any combination thereof, is the root cause of desire and suffering in the world. At the same time, consciously and mindfully focusing upon and contemplating the impermanence of the skandhas can bring the practitioner to the experience of Nirvana through the elimination of self-ness. From the Sutra:

> Avalokita, The Holy Lord and Bodhisattva, was moving in the deep course of the Wisdom which has gone beyond. He looked down from on high, He beheld but five heaps, and he saw that in their own-being they were empty.

> Here, Sariputra, form is emptiness and the very emptiness is form; emptiness doesn't differ from form, form doesn't differ from emptiness; whatever is form, that is emptiness, whatever is emptiness, that is form, the same is true of feelings, perceptions, impulses and consciousness....

> Therefore, Sariputra, it's because of his non-attainment that a Bodhisattva, through having relied on the Perfection of Wisdom, dwells without thought-coverings. In the absence of thought-coverings he has

not been made to tremble, he has overcome what can upset, and in the end he attains to Nirvana.[21]

Remarkably, the Gnostic *Secret Book of John* (NHL) also lists five "powers," or Archons, that govern the interaction of the human with the Kosmos:

> The one who governs perceptions: Archendekta
> The one who governs reception: Deitharbathas
> The one who governs imagination: Oummaa
> The one who governs integration: Aachiaram
> The one who governs impulse: Riaramnacho.

The skandhas and the governors of perception have an almost one-to-one correspondence, though we present them in a different order. This isn't to suggest that the author of SJn was familiar with the skandhas

---

[21] http://www.dharmanet.org/HeartSutra.htm

or that this was originally intended; however, it's certainly an interesting thematic correspondence:

Form: Rupa:: Impulse: Riaramnacho

Sensation: Vedana:: Reception: Deitharbathas

Perception: Sanna:: Perception: Archendekta

Mental Formations: Sankhara:: Imagination: Oumma

Consciousness: Vinanna:: Integration: Aachiaram

Since the qualities of these Archons are so patently concerned with phenomenology, and as the Buddhist skandhas are an aggregation of various experiences as perceived by humans through the senses but are not essentially real, so the Archons also represent unreal experiences within the World of Forms which lead the human into pleasure, desire, grief and fear. Once again, from SJn:

The four chief demons are:
Ephememphi, associated with pleasure,
Yoko, associated with desire,
Nenentophni, associated with distress,
Blaomen, associated with fear.

Their mother is Esthesis-Zouch-Epi-Ptoe.

Out from these four demons come passions:
From distress arises
Envy, jealousy, grief, vexation,
Discord, cruelty, worry, mourning.

From pleasure comes much evil
And unmerited pride,
And so forth.

From desire comes
Anger, fury, bitterness, outrage, dissatisfaction
And so forth.

From fear emerges
Horror, flattery, suffering, and shame.

Of course, there is no indication within Sethian thought that the Self doesn't exist. Indeed, the Archons involved in the creation and perception of the ephemeral world serve to occlude the Self at their center. *This doesn't mean that invisible aliens are crawling all over your soul; these are not "Body thetans."* They are, instead, the impermanent things that impede one's ability to experience the psychospiritual state we call "dwelling in gnosis." They're the roadblock on the path to self-knowledge, and through mindful contemplation on them, one doesn't discover that there is no self, but instead discovers that essential spark of the Universal Self that exists under the surface of the World of Forms.

Regardless of the tradition, the idea is that as we accumulate experiences during life, we also accumulate roadblocks to the Pleromic worldview in the form of an aggregate of accidents. Let's think of this aggregate as a False Self, or, as the Sethians might have had it, a *Counterfeit Spirit*. This doppelganger is the way we present ourselves to the World of Forms, **as determined by the World of Forms.** It's a duplicate of our outward appearance, and it's responsible for the idea that, in a real way, we're addicted to the concept that "what you see is what you get." **Again, this isn't necessarily the ancient Gnostic understanding of the Counterfeit Spirit.**[22]

---

[22] For a good overview of what the ancients may have thought, check out "What is the Counterfeit Spirit?" by Miguel Conner. http://www.examiner.com/article/what-is-the-counterfeit-spirit

As we tend only to interact with the False Self, we perceive the accidents as the real deal– we tend to mistake a person's counterfeit spirit for his or her essential self. Thus, when we generalize individuals based on any externality or expression we aren't really coming to any kind of truth about that individual, but instead to whatever Archonic feature of the World of Forms has contributed these accidents to that person's being. We do the same thing when we are overly self-critical: "I wish I weren't so fat/short/tall/dumb." These are all aspects of the counterfeit spirit, not the essential Self.

The point is, people are not "evil," or "good," or "colored," or "smart," or "stupid," or anything really, other than themselves. People may *do* good things, or *do* evil things, but essentially we are all uniquely individual underneath the kipple that piles upon us within the World of Forms. When we assign individuals the attributes of generalities, we are therefore mixing up cause and effect in a nasty way. And, when we extrapolate the actions of someone's counterfeit spirit and apply them to a generality, we're also not really understanding cause and effect.

Another, simpler way to put it would be as follows:

Politicians are not stupid. Sometimes politicians do stupid stuff. However, just because some politicians do stupid stuff doesn't mean that everyone in politics should be vilified. What it means is that **we should see the cause of the problems politics generates as the intersection of the individual Counterfeit Spirit and the Archonic Power that is "Politics."** Religious people are not good, or evil. Sometimes religious people do good things, and sometimes they do things that are evil. However, just because some religious people are assholes doesn't mean we have to apply that generalization to all religious people. What it means is that individuals should be judged solely on their own merits, keeping in mind that *all we can ever really perceive of a person is his or her doppelganger*.

So how best to approach this problem-- and it's a HUGE problem-- without falling back into wishy-washy moderation or existential inactivity? The only real way would be to honestly assess cause and effect in any given interpersonal situation, which can only be done by stripping the individuals with whom we come into contact of as many accidents as possible (here I mean "accidents" in the philosophical sense, as an "attribute which may or may not pertain to something's essential nature").

I think one of the essential messages of many enlightened individuals is, Most people are pretty okay. Sometimes they get involved in stupid stuff, but it's the stuff that's stupid, not the person.

In theory, confronting the counterfeit spirit, both within one's own person and in other people, seems like a fairly straightforward proposition. But **it gets way more complicated and dirty in practice**. Doesn't it always?

# Totally Reasonable

The idea that some kind of good God exists? **Totally reasonable.** At least, it seems more reasonable than the idea that existence is some weird, meaningless series of quantum events, that all of our experiences are purposeless chemical reactions, and that the life we live has no more import in space/time than that of a tardigrade. (I mean, if you're the kind of person who finds comfort in a cosmos devoid of meaning that churns along and spits out chemical eddies called "humans" who happen to interact with one another in a purely physical form and then vanish into background noise, that's your bag, but it seems pretty depressing to me.)

The idea that this good God created the universe as we currently experience it? **Totally unreasonable.** My poor little kid is sick with a high fever, and he's crying and miserable, and, at the moment, he's got it good: he was born an insured white male in a relatively prosperous nation to a pair of loving parents with steady incomes. What kind of God would endorse his tears, and endorse the tears of millions of other kids who don't have it as good as he does simply because they were born somewhere else, or born uninsured, or born and then abandoned? There is no argument you can make that a good God would knowingly allow countless children to suffer.

The idea that an Evil force opposes this good God, and is responsible for the suffering in the world? **Totally unreasonable**, if, indeed, this God created everything. Why would you go and do something like that? There isn't a single good argument one can make for giving one's self an opponent if one knows very well that one's opponent will cause others to suffer. I suppose if one wanted to challenge one's self, one might come up with an archenemy, a super-villain who could test one's abilities and self-worth. But if this super-villain could spread misery around, and if you couldn't do anything to prevent that misery, wouldn't the act of creating this super-villain be wildly irresponsible?

The idea that the God who created the universe as we currently experience it is imperfect? **Totally reasonable.** Really, if you're going down the path of theism, it's the only explanation that makes any reasonable sense. God itself is unwise; it's been abandoned by Wisdom, or refuses to accept it. Obviously, this God isn't totally cruel; there's a lot of beauty and happiness in the world, and it can be a fantastic place to live. It just doesn't seem to have any kind of consistent moral head on its shoulders.

So what, then, of our relationship to God? What is a **totally reasonable** way to look at our place in a theistic cosmos if God itself is imperfect? Perhaps the most reasonable way to look at God in relation to us is to ask the question, **what if God is, like us, imperfectly striving towards self-knowledge?**

After all, if we were created in God's image, and God is imperfect, then it makes perfect sense that our desire to know ourselves and to understand ourselves mirrors God's own desire to do so? And, if this is the case, then doesn't it also make sense that the best way for God to come to its own self-knowledge is through the creation of observers and experiencers within itself?

Perhaps, and I'm riffing on some old themes here, perhaps in the God's own Gnostic Way, in its desire to know itself, it continually sends imperfect segments of its own greater Consciousness into the realm of experience. These segments, existing outside of space and time, are unrestricted by them. These segments, through interaction with the components of the material world such as DNA, are the way in which God comes to know itself.

This forced subjective experience accounts for the perception of the Universe as a region of insanity, a place from which we must escape. The question then becomes, how much of the ego survives us? Does it choose where to manifest next? Can it choose the path of no return, and an eternal peace in the Limitless Light? Or, is it something we have no control over? Or indeed, does it depend upon our actions here on Earth? If we're 'good,' or find the 'Way,' does that mean we go to Heaven? Can some of us return as boddhisatvas to assist others on their journeys? Yes, yes and yes. All of these things are possible, and none, because there is only one consciousness, experiencing itself subjectively, unlimited by space and time.

Practically speaking, it means that after death, one's consciousness can re-manifest in any portion of the Universe's subjective experience. I could die tomorrow and be reborn again within my body. I could die tomorrow and be reborn as an amoeba, or as any other human now living or dead, past or present, or as a cephalopodan life form orbiting a distant star. I could die tomorrow and be reborn as you, the reader. Conversely you could die tomorrow and be reborn on September 2, 1975 to a young couple in Florida who would name you Jeremy Puma. The experience seems limited by space/time, but nothing suggests that reincarnation into the subjective occurs in a linear fashion.

If this is the case, memories of 'past lives' are merely memories of different subjective encounters with the World of Forms. I might remember a 'past life' as Napoleon, but so might you, and we'd both be correct; our objective consciousnesses both experienced the life of Napoleon, so why not?

There is no need for a Hell. Hitler died and became every single one of his victims, had to experience every evil ever committed by his followers from the other end. They didn't realize they were Hitler when it happened; does that make it any better, or even worse? Each of them was reborn within the consciousness of Hitler and perpetrated these crimes against themselves, who were, in turn, Hitler. There is one experiencer, one recipient of all the good and ill produced by the subjective realm, one objective consciousness that seeks to learn about itself by experiencing each and every subjective manifestation of itself.

This accounts for the perception of selflessness as 'good' and selfishness as 'evil,' though again, these are limited terms. Simply put, what you do unto even the least of humanity you do unto the Christ within because what you do unto even the least of humanity you do to yourself. Lie, cheat, steal, kill? You're lying to, cheating, stealing from and murdering yourself. Murder is suicide, and vice-versa. Don't just consider how another person feels or reacts to your actions—consider how you would feel if you were reborn as that person, and had to share her experiences, her highs and lows, her happinesses and tragedies.

Eschatological concerns are of course implied. One would assume that once every manifestation of itself has been experienced by the Universe, it becomes whole, healed, and no longer needs to break itself into pieces. That may indeed be the case, but that's only how it looks to us from the realm of limitation. Beyond space/time, the entire process is already complete, and the process is just beginning. The End of Time happened yesterday; the Universe will be created tomorrow. Time isn't linear **or** cyclical; these are human concepts. Time is an illusory, subjective experience of an amorphous process of discovery, the gnosis of the universe itself.

What better Heaven than to exist as the Universal consciousness, dancing through its manifestations in total Freedom, be they imperfect or limited? It's a grand adventure with infinite possibilities and infinite choices, a game of perpetual exploration and discovery and self-knowledge with very little in the way of correct or incorrect. **The 'goal' is simple: know, know, know!** Only in knowing one's self, for one's self, does the individual achieve enlightenment, and **only in knowing itself for itself does the God become complete.** To me, this is the ultimate message of all gnostic streams of thought and the underlying basis for everything from ontology to morality.

It would be easy to sentimentalize this concept, as so many have done, into a "we are all one everything happens for a reason universal peace and love" philosophy, but to do so would be to ignore the realistic limitations of subjective experience. **We are all one, but that "One" is limited by the subjective realm**. We do create our own reality, but from beyond the ego and as a collective of individual experiencers, not as individuals within the realm of limitations. "Creating one's reality" is well and good, but it's a concept limited to those untouched by tragedy and is utterly useless to, say, someone who has lost h/er entire village to a tsunami. "We are all one" is well and good, but it's a concept limited to those who choose to ignore the value of individual experience and self-knowledge. "Peace and love" are well and good, but they're concepts limited to those who have never had close relatives murdered at the hands of a death squad.

We are not God; or, if we are, we are a tiny and powerless segment of an imperfect and unknowable God. **Claiming that one is**

**"one with God" means accepting that one is imperfect, unknowing, and slight.**

There are three virtues implied by this outlook: compassion and humility and **radical inquiry**. Our fragmentary nature requires compassion for others as extensions of our selves, segments of the universe. This same fragmentary nature requires humility as an admission that our experience is limited and subjective, and the subjective experiences of others may not be more true or more false than those of our own. These limitations require constant questioning in order to allow the universe to experience itself more fully. None of these three necessitate "peace" or "love" or anything we usually associate with goodness, but peace and love et al are natural extensions of these virtues, not vice-versa as some assume.

Conversely, we can understand "evil" as viewing the limitation as the whole, viewing other individual fragments as objects without value. Acts which restrict the individual and subjective universal experience serve only to limit the universe's ability to know itself, and to delay the redemptive process.

"Good" and "evil" are symptoms, not causes, and are better understood in terms of "sanity" and "insanity."

Of course, these things only exist in space and time, in subjective experience. One will argue that since the process isn't linear, that the universe is already redeemed at some point, why should it matter whether we choose "good" or "evil" within this manifestation? Such a question makes little sense; we exist as we exist, limited, and are subject to the actions of one another. As a practical matter, this timeless redemption **requires** sanity, and even though it's already healed in some timeless form, this is due to the acts of compassion, humility and perpetual questioning of its fragmented parts. Sure, you could go out and do something horrifying to someone and it would have little effect on the final state of the universe, but it would have negative effect on **you** as an eventual/possible manifestation of your victim. On many levels, it's a utilitarian matter, one of the few.

What about combating those who commit evil acts? Protesting governments? Confronting bullies? Jailing criminals? The only possible way to combat an act of evil is to lead by example, displaying compassion, humility, and a willingness to question, and to remember that no one can change anyone else's mind.

The most valuable interactions one has are with those in one's circle of direct experience. If every single person decided to be more compassionate to, to be a little more humble around, to be more willing to ask questions of and for one's family, one's friends, one's neighbors, one's coworkers, then nobody would need to petition governments or jail criminals. Idealistic, yes, but no more idealistic than the absurd theory that enough people's signatures will cause a politician to change h/er mind for any reason. Idealism is a necessity not because the best-case scenario will occur, but in order that idealist visions remain within discourse.

Let's face it; we'll never really know anything, but maybe this is by design. Maybe our ignorance, as a reflection of the ignorance of God, is a step towards the redemption of God itself. Maybe we're here to help it along. And that seems **totally reasonable** to me.

Even in the most meaningless particle of earth and sky I hear God crying out: "Help me!" – Nikos Kazantzakis, *The Saviors of God*

# Christmas is About Presents

I was listening to National Public Radio the other day, and a caller asked what seems like a really reasonable question: why Christmas, and not Easter? I mean, Easter is the BIG day, right? It's the holiest of holidays on the Christian calendar, symbolizes the return of God to Earth; He Is Risen, etc. So why don't we have months of Easter commercials and Easter lights and Easter carols and specials and movies about people finding love on Easter underneath the Easter basket?

The hosts answered with some rather underwhelming thoughts about how we all have birthdays and everybody thinks babies are cute and what a good story, but underlined that the history of the celebration as we know it is fairly complex. I think the reason is a little simpler, and a little more primal. I think that **Christmas is about how awesome it is to get presents.**

Now wait, before you get all "yikes! Materialism, commercialism, Linus's speech, you fiend!" let me explain what I mean. Think about your best Christmas memories, and how amazing Christmas can be, and you'll likely include at least a couple of things you remember from childhood. I remember, for instance, the old steamer trunk we used to store our decorations, and how exciting it would be to open it on the day the tree arrived, and the books it contained that only came out once a year. I remember carolling and driving around looking at lights. But, in a large way, **I really remember the anticipation of waking up on Christmas morning and running out to the living room to see what was left under the tree.**

That sense of **anticipation**, the sense of **hope**, was always sweeter than the actual revelation of the contents of the wrapped boxes and packages strewn across the living room floor. And this is what I mean by **Christmas is about how awesome it is to get presents.** It's about the entire season, the journey that begins on Thanksgiving and ends when the last present is opened. It's about looking forward to a delightful dinner and a day off of work. It's about having to wait without knowing exactly what you'll get. **Will it be disappointing? Will it be awesome? EEEE, I can't sleep!!!**

Because, you see, this is the message of the original Christmas story: a couple in the ancient Near East wander around because they're ordered to by the government, and even though she's pregnant, they keep getting turned away from inn to inn (what a nifty metaphor for life in the World of Forms!). Eventually, they find a place to stay, and it's a place that's pretty dirty, a stinky old stable full of animals (no matter what Benedict XVI says, there most certainly were donkeys and cows and camels and such), and then Mary gives birth to a tiny baby who will eventually... wait for it... WAIT FOR IT... SAVE THE WHOLE WORLD! Yow!

See, it's all about anticipation! It's all about hope! It's intended to tell us that no matter how shitty things get down here in the World of Forms, no matter how long we have to wait, the True God has a plan. It may take some time, and it may not turn out exactly the way we expected it to, but for those of us in the know (*wink wink I'm looking at you!*), the sweetness of anticipation and the hope of the redemption of the World of Forms makes putting up with all of these Archons totally worthwhile.

Obviously people think that the three kings (who really should be called 'the group of a few astrologers') brought the first Christmas gifts-- all that gold and incense (say, what happened to all of that stuff, anyhow? Wouldn't that have been useful to a carpenter's family in ancient Palestine? Did Joseph maybe keep it for himself, use it to supplement the family's income for a while? Er, sorry, losing track here...)-- all that gold and incense weren't the first gift. The first Christmas gift was the promise represented by that little baby resting in the animal's food, the promise that even though his power is limited here in this realm of imperfection, **he's got a** *plan,* **and it** *just might work,* **so we have something to hope for.**

So don't get all uppity with kids who are really excited about getting stuff for Christmas. It's okay to hope that something terrific is under the tree, wrapped in paper– in fact, **that's what it's all about.**

# Everyday Apocalypse

The students asked him, "How will everything end?"

The teacher said, "You don't even know how everything began and you want to know how it'll end? The end and the beginning are in the same place. It's great for you if you're there at the beginning; if you can do that, you'll know how things are gonna end, and you won't die."

- *Brother Tom's Miracle Book of Signs and Wonders*

---

Well well well. It was going to be AMAZING: people were gonna be nicer, maybe get magic powers; Mayan Timelords like Pacal Votan would be zipping around in UFOs; we'd all be made of light or some such thing and be able to read directly from the Akashic Records. Yep, it was gonna be one big PAR-TAY. And, hey, if anything like that **did** happen, it would've been pretty great, wouldn't it?

O'course, the reasonable among us know that the whole 2012 apocalypse thing was more of a marketing scheme than anything else, a way for New Age jerks and white fratboy neo-Messiahs like Daniel Pinchbeck to sell books and make money exploiting the nuanced and fascinating belief systems of ACTUAL INDIGENOUS CULTURES. Although it would be pretty rockin' if we woke up and the Galactic Umbilical Cord connected us all to Hunab Ku and we could eat all the pasta we wanted without getting fat, we just ended up going to work like usual, only we got to read two dozen "wakka wakka wakka" stories on CNN.com about how it wasn't actually the Mayan Apocalypse and how KA-RAY-AY-AY-ZY! people were for thinking such things.

The problem is, telling people the End of the World is Nigh has ACTUAL, REAL WORLD EFFECTS, and they're not all good. Remember Adam Lanza, the perpetrator in the Sandy Hook massacre? His mother was part of the "Doomsday Preppers" "Movement" (is this really a movement? Sounds like another marketing scheme to me...), which is why she had guns stockpiled, and you know she's not the only one out there. Let's face it: every gun in the underground bunker of someone who sincerely believes the End is upon us, whether the rapture or just a run-of-the-mill economic collapse, is another mass murder waiting to happen.

Hell, the "End" that these folks are worrying about can even be something less global. Opponents of gun control are worried that "They" are going to come and take away all of their guns. So what do these folks do? Why, they buy more guns, of course. And unprecedented gun sales means (yay!) unprecedented potential for more mass murders.

It's easy to blame these people for being crazy, but it's a little more complicated than that. We touched on this during the whole Harold Camping debacle in 2011, when everyone was making fun of the silly Christians for buying into the idea that the apocalypse was just around the corner just because Camping said so.

Really, though, it was all kinds of hilarious when you first heard it, the world ending on May 21, 2011. "Gee, better put the date into the ol' iPhone calendar," etc. "Haha, those crazy (choose one: Christians/American

Protestants/Fundies), let's hope they do get sucked up into Heaven so we don't have to deal with them. THOSE GUYS ARE JERKS!" But I started thinking about it, thinking about all of the people who actually believe in the obviously ridiculous premise that a bunch of people will be sucked up into the sky tomorrow and the rest of us will fight it out here and then get dropped into a good, old-fashioned lake of fire. And I thought, man, it must really be nice to believe in something that fiercely, with such earnest sincerity that you give up everything for an ideal (which, by the bye, is the basic gist of a lot of what Jesus actually said you should do). It would take a pretty strong will to be able to do that. Even if I think the idea is absurd, I can't imagine ever having that kind of moxie.

And then I thought, not all of these people can be "stupid" or "ignoramuses." They believe some weird stuff which is a little more easily proven false than the average weird stuff. But, how many people do I know who believe that politicians have the best interest of the public in mind? How many believe that some bread and wine turn into God on Sunday? How many believed that something remarkable would happen in December of 2012? How many believe that the world **will** end as described in the Bible, but we just don't know when it will happen? How many believed that enormous banks would assist them with low-interest mortgages? How many of these ideas are equally absurd on the face of things, and how many people would be willing to give up so much because of them? Really, the fool isn't the one who gives up everything for her beliefs. The fool is the one who believes without being willing to make any kind of investment in that belief.

For the people duped-- however unwittingly-- by Mr. Camping, who was likely quite sincere, this wasn't a farce, it was a tragedy. Although many likely remained in the fold, and although Mr. Camping 'recalculated,' and declared that the Rapture is postponed due to the faith of his followers, there were a good many people who were devastated that Sunday. Not only did they lose their fortunes and friends and worldly things, they likely lost their **faith**, the core of their beings. These people are in no way deserving of ridicule, any more than those who lost their houses, jobs, fortunes and families due to the predatory lending crisis and the subsequent economic downturn. In both cases, people put their faith in something larger, and in both cases, became the victims. That's not funny, it's sad.

So what can we do? To me, one solution would be to reframe the idea of the Apocalypse, to focus more on the idea that "the End of Things" is something built into the fabric of the World of Forms, and is an internal process, a method to interact with Living Intelligence, not a hypostatic concept.

"There he goes again. What are you going on about this time, Puma, you jargony bastard?"

I mean, check out that quote at the top of the post: we don't know when the hell the end of the world is going to happen. We don't even know where the world came from! Fact is, the only constant in the World of Forms is change. The world you think you know today will be TOTALLY DIFFERENT tomorrow; the world you know this hour will pass away the next. If you don't know what I mean, just ask the people of Newtown whether or not their world ended in December of 2012, whether a mountain of fire descended upon their community and a black horseman rode through their streets.

The Apocalypse isn't something that happens in space/time. It's a symbolic interface we can use to interact with the often violent change inherent to the World of Forms. The End-Times Resurrection is a way for us to understand the role of the Christos and Sophia within our personal lives. A great passage about this process can be found in "All About Being Born Again (The Treatise on the Resurrection)":

> So what does it mean to be resurrected? It's always for those who are born again while they're still alive. You remember reading about Jesus that Elijah and Moses showed their faces to him, but don't think it was some kind of trick. It's no trick; it's TRUTH! Actually, it makes more sense to say that the World is a Trick, rather than being Born Again through our Saviour Christ Jesus! So what am I really telling you? The living are gonna die. How can they not know it's a trick? The rich are poor, and the kings are tossed out.

Everything changes. The World is a Trick! It's worth repeating!

The resurrection, though, is no trick; it's the solid truth. It's learning all about what's real, and how things change and become new. Something rotten becomes fresh, and the dark gets lightened, and the Pleroma fills up the World of Forms. These are all symbolic ways to talk about being born again. Jesus Christ redeems.[23]

The Apocalypse is an everyday occurrence. It happens all the time, every second. It's happening right now, inside you.

This is the lesson we can take from the End Times narratives: if things are always changing here in the World of Forms, and could potentially get a lot worse, doesn't it make sense to love one another, to interface with reality using Reason and Wisdom, to focus on what's real and valuable in life?

Look, we can't predict the future. It's a bad idea to even try, because you'll just end up anxious. What we **can** do, is to try to live as

[23] http://www.strangeanimal.net/thisway/?p=483

though the next second will bring annihilation and rebirth. It's kind of clichéd, but the Apocalypse can teach us a special kind of self-knowledge: the knowledge of what we would do if we knew the end happened next. If we all blinked out of existence ten minutes from now, would you be satisfied with the life you've led? What would you regret not having done? What would you be happy about? Who would you want to tell that one thing to? Shouldn't you go ahead and do that? Your answers to these questions are your resurrected body.

The alternative is living in fear, and that never gets us anywhere. You can stockpile guns, but when you do that, you're storing up death. You can hoard food, but when you do that, you're just creating spoilage. What you can save up that has value is what you'll use in the very final seconds prior to the end of being, when you won't have enough time to shoot a weapon or eat a can of beans. You can save up relationships, you can save up self-knowledge.

The world just ended! Oop, it was just Reborn! Oh heck, it ended again! Now it's back, and it ends again in just a second. What are you going to do about it?

# The Case for a Phildickian Religious Movement

I.

The November 2012 release of Philip K Dick's *Exegesis* produced a trickle of disdainful analyses of his philosophical and spiritual pursuits, and trite comparisons to L. Ron Hubbard. Rather than address these fairly puerile criticisms of PKD's attempts at understanding the nature of reality (He Was Crazy! He Was On Amphetamines! Therefore He Was A Crank!), an undertaking that would necessitate far more time or energy than would be worth it, I think a discussion on the merits of a practical Phildickian approach to religion and philosophy is long overdue. I think many members of the community of PKD admirers like to tiptoe around this question, even as we all "personally" feel as though PKD's writings address our spiritual concerns far better than 99% of everything else that's out there.

So, why not start the discussion? After all, we coined the phrase "Phildickian Gnosticism" way back when most people only knew PKD from Bladerunner and Total Recall. Although we've transcended the categorical inconsistencies of "Gnosticism," we remain dedicated to the work of PKD, so why not take it a step further? Let's explore some reasons that PKD, as a religious figure, makes a certain amount of sense.

**Philip K. Dick was a prophet**. It's not that the guy was a prophet in the 'predict the future' sense– his work just as often missed the mark (vide Joe Chip's fashion choices in *UBIK*). It's that the issues he addresses are those that concern humanity in the modern world. What is Reality? What is the role of technology in society? What is the role of Power in government, or in interpersonal relationships? The Biblical prophets attempted to address these very same questions in their own cultural milieu, but a few thousand years have passed since the time of Jeremiah and Daniel. In the 'fiction' of PKD, we find the same concerns of the biblical prophets: the same intense warnings that if we can't get our shit together, bad things are going to happen to us, and the same urgent concern for the fate of his fellows.

**PKD was a visionary**. Regardless of whether you think it was Temporal Lobe Epilepsy, amphetamine use or actual contact with a super-intelligent satellite (or a little of each), PKD had visions that most certainly had real-world implications in his life, and the lives of others. He had a connection to something deeper that revealed itself in religious and psychological terms. he translated this vision into work which has touched so many of us so deeply that its visionary quality cannot be denied.

**PKD provides a consistent mythos**. VALIS. Palmer Eldritch. Zebra. The Palm Tree Garden. The Black Iron Prison. The Homoplasmate. Need I say more? Suffice to say that these themes, fairly consistent in various incarnations of his work since the beginning of his career, provide a standard semiotic set through which to interface with "reality." This mythos is also exceptionally well-suited to the modern era, explaining sacramental practice in terms of information theory and the structure of the universe in terms of holographic projections.

**PKD left a wealth of source material.** Between the novels, short stories, philosophical work and transcripts from his talks, those of us interested in his work have a massive collection of data through which to mine. No doubt the two-volume Exegesis release added to this source material, but even if it had never seen the light of day, there would be enough material to maintain a movement indefinitely. As a sub-category to this item, consider the incredible volume of popular themes that his work has inspired.

**PKD always asked questions**. In his *Exegesis*, the guy practiced an almost ultimate form of the Path of Radical Inquiry. Never content with a single explanation for his experiments, he struggled and played with ideas and constantly second-guessed his own experiences until his death. Any PKD-based modern movement that will contribute anything of value to society must also constantly be willing to second-guess its own motives.

**PKD was radically ecumenical.** Although his philosophical influences were primarily Christian and Greek, one can also find signs of Taoism, Buddhism, Existentialism and Humanism in his work, often expounded upon in one place, only to be dismissed in the next. It's fair to say that those of us who appreciate the philosophical value of his work recognize that there's "something for everyone."

However....

**PKD's outlook is realistic**. In spite of the fact that he wrote mostly scifi, much of his work is firmly grounded in the vagaries of the world of illusion in which we're firmly ensconced. He quite convincingly illustrates, again and again, that this is kind of a shitty place for us to be. There's no room in PKD's universe for the kind of New Agey namby-pamby nonsense of disposable spirituality or false garage churches.

And yet....

**PKD was unapologetically imperfect**. The guy pulled some odious stunts (denouncing Stanislaw Lem to the FBI as a Commie?). His personal life was a case-study of someone unable to come to grips with some of the most basic aspects of interpersonal relationships. He was paranoid, pretentious, and had lousy taste in modern music. He was, in short, one of us.

Finally, and perhaps most importantly....

**PKD's core values are kindness, compassion and love**. These are, in his work, what makes humans human, and it's impossible to argue that this is an essential message desperately necessary at the moment. In the end, these are the core values necessary if we wish to break free of the Black Iron Prison and find ourselves within the cool oasis of the Palm Tree Garden.

II.

What kind of "primary texts" would a Phildickian religion use? We have a wealth of textual information available from the mind of Philip K. Dick himself. Although we will assume the reader has a basic familiarity with his works of science fiction, of far more interest to our discussion are his exegetical materials. Over the course of his career, Dick produced-- according to rumor-- about 8,000 pages of personal attempts at understanding his experiences, only a fraction of which has been published as *The Exegesis of Philip K. Dick*. Fascinating, frustrating, profound and contradictory, the *Exegesis* delivers a powerful insight into a struggling mind, but is far too difficult to begin with for this discussion. It would be like attempting to discuss orthodox Christianity using the collected works of St. Augustine instead of opting for the Nicene Creed.

Rather than delve into the complexities of the *Exegesis*, of primary interest to our very basic discussion are a few of his more prevalent and available distillations of his work, all of which can be found online via a simple Google search. The most essential summary is the "Tractates Cryptica Scriptura," appended to the semi-autobiographical novel *VALIS*. This remarkable document (from here forward referred to as "TCS") contains the foundational philosophies of Philip K. Dick, and provide us with an excellent starting point for our discussion. Originally published in 1981, a year before his death, it contains what I believe is the most succinct summary of the Phildickian way. Unfortunately, due to the vagaries of copyright law, I'm unable to include the TCS here in full; however, I encourage the reader to seek out this incredible document for herself. The quotations that follow are from the 1981 Bantam Books edition.

What does the TCS tell us about the nature of reality, and how we might interpret it within a spiritual context? We might balk at some of the more outlandish features found in the TCS, such as the references to Ikhnaton and the three-eyed aliens that appear to the Dogon, but for now let's focus on the essential messages regarding reality and the nature of humanity. In my opinion, if we strip down the essential message contained in the TCS, we find something like this:

**1. There is an ultimate Mind, which is our highest concern:**

> *One Mind there is; but under it two principles contend.*
> *(TCS 1)*

**2. The reality in which we find ourselves is dualistic. Two principles (Light and Dark, Spirit and Matter, etc.) are contending with one another, and this contention results in the illusion of change within the cosmos:**

*The Mind lets in the light, then the dark,
in interaction; so time is generated. At
the end Mind awards victory to the light;
time ceases and the Mind is complete.
He causes things to look different so it
would appear time has passed.
Matter is plastic in the face of mind.*
*(TCS 2-5)*

3. **All that truly exists is living
information, which the Mind
communicates, and which we, its portions,
"hypostasize" ("make real"):**

*The universe is information and we are
stationary in it, not three-dimensional
and not in space or time. The
information fed to us we hypostatize
into the phenomenal world.*
*(TCS 14)*

4. **Mind is attempting to
communicate with us, its segments, via
this living information, but we somehow
lost the ability to comprehend what it's
telling us.**

*The Mind is not talking to us but by means of us. Its narrative passes through us and its sorrow infuses us irrationally. As Plato discerned, there is a streak of the irrational in the World Soul.*

*In Summary: thoughts of the brain are experienced by us as arrangements and rearrangements—change—in a physical universe; but in fact it is really information and information-processing which we substantialize. We do not merely see its thoughts as objects, but rather as the movement, or, more precisely, the placement of objects: how they become linked to one another. But we cannot read the patterns of arrangement; we cannot extract the information in it—i.e. it as information, which is what it is. The linking and relinking of objects by the Brain is actually a language, but not a language like ours (since it is addressing itself and not someone or something outside itself).*

*(TCS 35-36)*

**5.** Something went wrong; what should be a unity instead split into a duality. Now the universe consists of two parts, Forms I and II. Form I is whole, sensate, complete. Form II, in which we reside, is insane, delusional and subject to astral determinism. The world in which we reside is an unsuccessful attempt by a limited being to copy Form I:

> *The One was and was-not, combined, and desired to separate the was-not from the was. So it generated a diploid sac which contained, like an eggshell, a pair of twins, each an androgyny, spinning in opposite directions (the Yin and Yang of Taoism, with the One as the Tao). The plan of the One was that both twins would emerge into being (wasness) simultaneously; however, motivated by a desire to be (which the One implanted in both twins), the counter-clockwise twin broke through the sac and separated prematurely; i.e. before full term. This was the dark or Yin twin. Therefore it was defective. At full term the wiser twin emerged. Each*

*twin formed a unitary entelechy, a single living organism made of psyche and soma, still rotating in opposite directions to each other. The full term twin, called Form I by Parmenides, advanced correctly through its growth stages, but the prematurely born twin, called Form II, languished.*

*The next step in the One's plan was that the Two would become the Many, through their dialetic interaction. From them as hyperuniverses they projected a hologram-like interface, which is the pluriform universe we creatures inhabit. The two sources were to intermingle equally in maintaining our universe, but Form II continued to languish toward illness, madness and disorder. These aspects she projected into our universe.* (TCS 47)

**6. This confuses us into mistaking phenomena for reality, which is the true 'original sin.':**

*We should be able to hear this information, or rather narrative, as a neutral voice inside us. But something has gone wrong. All creation is a language and nothing but a language, which for some inexplicable reason we can't read outside and can't hear inside. So I say, we have become idiots. Something has happened to our intelligence. My reasoning is this: arrangement of parts of the Brain is language. We are parts of the Brain; therefore we are language. Why, then, do we not know this? We do not even know what we are, let alone what the outer reality is of which we are parts. The origin of the word "idiot" is the word "private." Each of us has become private, and no longer shares the common thought of the Brain, except at a subliminal level. Thus our real life and purpose are conducted below our threshold of consciousness.*
(TCS 37)

7. **The Empire, and its correlative, the Black Iron Prison, want to maintain this state of insanity:**

> *The Empire is the institution, the codification, of derangement; it is insane and imposes its insanity on us by violence, since its nature is a violent one.*
>
> *To fight the Empire is to be infected by its derangement. This is a paradox: whoever defeats a segment of the Empire becomes the Empire; it proliferates like a virus, imposing its form on its enemies. Thereby it becomes its enemies.*
>
> *(TCS 41-42)*

8. **The Mind, however, recognizes that we need to be healed, and has begun a rescue mission of sorts. Our healer, and savior, is Christ, through the medium of the Holy Spirit; PKD's soteriology is unquestionably Christian. As he says elsewhere in the Exegesis, "While such 'Enlightened' spiritual leaders as Zoroaster, Mani, Buddha, and Elijah can**

be regarded as receptors of the entity's total wisdom, Christ seems to have been an actual terminal of this computer-like entity, in which case he did not speak for it but was it. 'Was,' in this case, standing for 'consisted of a microform of it.'":

> Against the Empire is posed the living information, the plasmate or physician, which we know as the Holy Spirit or Christ discorporate. These are the two principles, the dark (the Empire) and the light (the plasmate). In the end, Mind will give victory to the latter. Each of us will die or survive according to which he aligns himself and his efforts with. Each of us contains a component of each. Eventually one or the other component will triumph in each human. Zoroaster knew this, because the Wise Mind informed him. He was the first savior. Four have lived in all. A fifth is about to be born, who will differ from the others: he will rule and he will judge us.
> Since the universe is actually composed of information, then it can be said that

information will save us. This is the saving gnosis which the Gnostics sought. There is no other road to salvation. However, this information—or more precisely the ability to read and understand this information, the universe as information—can only be made available to us by the Holy Spirit. We cannot find it on our own. Thus it is said that we are saved by the grace of God and not by good works, that all salvation belongs to Christ, who, I say, is a physician.

In seeing Christ in a vision I correctly said to him, "We need medical attention." In the vision there was an insane creator who destroyed what he created, without purpose; which is to say, irrationally. This is the deranged streak in the Mind; Christ is our only hope, since we cannot now call on Asklepios. Asklepios came before Christ and raised a man from the dead; for this act, Zeus had a Kyklopes slay him with a thunderbolt. Christ also was killed for what he had done: raising a man from the dead. Elijah brought a boy back to

*life and disappeared soon thereafter in a*
*whirlwind. "The Empire never ended."*
*(TCS 43-45)*

9. **Christ works through this Living Information, called the Plasmate, to cross-bond with humans who have access to this information, gnosis. Gnosis is not enlightenment, it is the receipt of living information. Once this information has been made available via sacraments, the recipient "awakens;" her memory is restored and she is no longer subject to amnesia. The "memory coil" becomes fixed and the ability to process information is restored:**

> *I term the Immortal One a plasmate,*
> *because it is a form of energy; it is living*
> *information. It replicates itself—not*
> *through information or in*
> *information—but as information.*
> *The plasmate can crossbond with a*
> *human, creating what I call a*
> *homoplasmate. This annexes the mortal*
> *human permanently to the plasmate.*
> *We know this as the "birth from above"*

or "birth from the Spirit." It was initiated by Christ, but the Empire destroyed all the homoplasmates before they could replicate.

In dormant seed form, the plasmate slumbered in the buried library of codices at Chenoboskion until 1945 C.E. This is what Jesus meant when he spoke elliptically of the "mustard seed" which, he said, "would grow into a tree large enough for birds to roost in." He foresaw not only his own death but that of all homoplasmates. He foresaw the codices unearthed, read, and the plasmate seeking out new human hosts to crossbond with; but he foresaw the absence of the plasmate for almost two thousand years.

As living information, the plasmate travels up the optic nerve of a human to the pineal body. It uses the human brain as a female host in which to replicate itself into its active form. This is an interspecies symbiosis. The Hermetic alchemists knew of it in theory from ancient texts, but could not duplicate it, since they could not locate the dormant,

*buried plasmate. Bruno suspected that the plasmate had been destroyed by the Empire; for hinting at this he was burned. "The Empire never ended."*
*(TCS 22-25)*

**10. Eventually, the Light will win. In the realm of Time, the contest continues, but in the realm of the Eternal, the Light has already been made victorious.**

*Within time, hyperuniverse II remains alive: "The Empire never ended." But in eternity, where the hyperuniverses exist, she has been killed—of necessity—by the healthy twin of hyperuniverse I, who is our champion. The One grieves for this death, since the One loved both twins; therefore the information of the Mind consists of a tragic tale of the death of a woman, the undertones of which generate anguish into all the creatures of the hologrammatic universe without their knowing why. This grief will depart when the healthy twin undergoes mitosis and the "Kingdom of God" arrives. The machinery for this*

*transformation—the procession within time from the Age of Iron to the Age of Gold—is at work now; in eternity it is already accomplished.*
(*TCS* 47)

This is the story told time and time again by PKD, in his *Exegesis*, in his works of fiction, in his correspondences. This is the story which would need to be the basis of a modern Phildickian religious movement. The remarkable thing about this story is its timelessness. PKD's philosophies correlate to everything from Taoism to Zen Buddhism to the Christian Gnostics to the ancient Greeks, but also to the Holographic Universe theory, Information Theory, depth psychology and the sometimes complicated abstractions of theoretical quantum physics.

This place we're in can be terrible, and is under the control of the forces of darkness. Everything we think we know about the way the world works, even down to the question of which direction time flows, is completely wrong. This place is spurious. However, rescue awaits! The Mind, in its infinite benevolence, is actively rectifying the ills of the world, and ultimately the Light's victory is a guarantee!

A more in-depth discussion of these ideas can be found in a section from the Exegesis titled "Cosmology and Cosmogony," also available online but, once again, far to long to reproduce here in its entirety. Nonetheless, those interested in PKD's philosophy as a religious model would do well to search it out, as it provides a more detailed analysis of the concepts presented in TCS. For example:

> ...[T]he Urgrund, the ultimate noos and maker, is secretly present in this cruel and spurious world. Being unaware of this, the artifact projecting this counterfeit world will continue heedlessly to inflict the needless suffering engendered by the mindless machinery (i.e. the causal processes) it customarily employs and has always employed. In my opinion the Urgrund has differentiated itself from being the One into plurality. Some fragments or "images" of it are certainly conscious of their identity; others perhaps are not.

*But as the level of pointless pain continues (and even increases), these separated "images" of the Urgrund will recollect themselves into conscious rebirth– equal to a sentence of death for the artifact or "regent."[24]*

Between TCS and "Cosmology and Cosmogony," PKD presents a complete philosophy influenced by many paradigms from human thought, without turning into the cultural imperialism or vague and bland pantheism of the New Age movement. It's a philosophy almost perfectly suited to the modern sensibility, and encompasses a wide range of questions and concerns many of us have about our place in the cosmos.

However, how does it apply to possible modern practice? What might he have meant by 'sacraments,' and how might we fit into the stories and ideas contained in TCS? How could someone who declares him or herself a "Valist" participate in the mysteries described by PKD?

---

[24] Dick, Philip K and Sutin, Lawrence. *The Shifting Realities of Philip K. Dick*. Vintage Books, 1996.

III.

Right off the bat, based on what we know about Dick and his approaches to philosophy and spirituality, we can conclude that there are no easy answers to the question of just what a practice of Phildickian philosophy (to which I'm going to refer as "Valism", after VALIS) would look like. As far as we know, PKD had no interest in starting a religion, or a religious movement. The major theme behind his spiritual life was a kind of applied supra-gnostic way, the Path of Radical Inquiry, a mysticism built upon a *Via Quaestio* where every possible answer is investigated, poured over, meditated upon.

PKD wrote science fiction, to be sure, but could be considered almost the diametrical opposite of the odious L. Ron Hubbard, who founded his own "religion" based on answers he'd already determined.

The practices we list below are guidelines, personal interpretations of how PKD's experiences can work towards enriching one's own religious life. Setting any of them in stone would certainly be counter to the Dickian spirit of Radical Inquiry, but as general approaches to practice, they seem to run consistently through Valism and could be a good starting point.

## 1. Sacramental Practice

Philip K. Dick was unquestionably a Christian, though certainly idiosyncratic. He referred to himself as an Episcopalian, attended church, and was close friends with Episcopalian Bishop James Pike. Claims that PKD was somehow opposed to organized religion-- or Christianity in general-- seem fairly baseless. Indeed, sacramental practice is perhaps one of the primary means through which Valism could be expressed which can be supported by PKD's own writing.

The very nature of his ideologies, as inconsistent as they could be, depended upon the idea of an inbreaking Savior, Jesus Christ, Living Information, descending into the Black Iron Prison in which we are trapped. The practice of sacramentalism is a lower-level (Form II) representation of this inbreaking. As VALIS, the Salvific Intelligence, beams the Living Information into the human form, so sacramental practice represents the activation of this information within the segment of time in which we are trapped.

There is something to be said for *ad hoc* sacramentalism based upon personal inspiration. Take, for example, the following autobiographical account from *VALIS*, Chap. 12 (wonderfully recreated in the film version of Radio Free Albemuth):

> I remembered back to an incident-more than an incident-involving my son Christopher. In March 1974 during the time that VALIS overruled me, held control of my mind, I had conducted a correct and complex initiation of Christopher into the ranks of the immortals. VALIS's medical knowledge had saved Christopher's physical life, but VALIS had not ended it there.
>
> This was an experience which I had treasured. It had been in utter stealth, concealed even from my son's mother.
>
> First I had fixed a mug of hot chocolate. Then I had fixed a hot dog on a bun with the usual trimmings;

Christopher, young as he was, loved hot dogs and warm chocolate.

Seated on the floor in Christopher's room with him, I-or rather VALIS in me, as me-had played a game. First, I jokingly held the cup of chocolate up, over my son's head; then, as if by accident, I had splashed warm chocolate on his head, into his hair. Giggling, Christopher had tried to wipe the liquid off; I had of course helped him. Leaning toward him, I had whispered:

"In the name of the Son, the Father, and the Holy Spirit." No one heard me except Christopher. Now, as I wiped the warm chocolate from my hair, I inscribed the sign of the cross on his forehead. I had now baptized him and now I confirmed him; I did so, not by the authority of the church, but by the authority of the living plasmate in me: VALIS himself. Next I said to my son, "Your secret name, your Christian name, is-" And I told him what it was. Only he and I are ever to know; he an I and VALIS.

Next, I took a bit of bread from the hot dog bun and held it forth; my son-still a baby, really-opened his mouth like a little bird, and I placed the bit of bread on it. We seemed, the two of us, to be sharing a meal; an ordinary simple, common meal.

For some reason it seemed essential-quite crucial-that he take no bite of the hot dog meat itself. Pork could not be eaten under these circumstances; VALIS filled me with this urgent knowledge.

As Christopher started to close his mouth to chew on the bit of bread, I presented him with the mug of warm chocolate. To my surprise-being so young he still drank normally from his bottle, never from a cup-he reached eagerly to take the mug; as he took it, lifted it to his lips and drank from it, I said, "This is my blood and this is my body."

My little son drank, and I took the mug back. The greater sacraments had been accomplished. Baptism, then confirmation, then the most holy sacrament of all, the Eucharist: Sacrament of the Lord's Supper.

"The Blood of out Lord Jesus Christ, which was shed for thee, preserve thy body and soul unto everlasting life. Drink this in remembrance that Christ's blood was shed for thee, and be thankful."

This moment is most solemn of all. The priest himself has become Christ who offers his body and blood to the faithful, by a divine miracle.

Most people understand that in he miracle of transubstantiation the wine (or warm chocolate) becomes the Sacred Blood, and the wafer (or bit of hot dog bun) becomes the Sacred Body, but few people even within the churches realize that the figure who stands before them holding the cup is their Lord, living now. Time has been overcome. We are back almost two thousand years: we are not in Santa Ana, California, USA, but in Jerusalem, about 35 C.E.

What I had seen in March 1974 when I saw the superimposition of ancient Rome and modern California consisted of an actual witnessing of what is normally seen by the inner eyes of faith only.

My double-exposure experience had confirmed the literal – not merely figurative – truth of the miracle of the mass.

As I have said, the technical term for this is anamnesis: the loss of forgetfulness; which is to say, the remembering of the Lord and the Lord's Supper.

I was present that day, the last time the disciples sat at table. You may believe me; you may not. Sed per spiritum sanctum dico; haec veritas est. *Mihi crede et mecum in aeternitate vivebis.*

My Latin is probably faulty, but what I am trying to say, haltingly, is: "But I speak by means of the Holy Spirit; that is so. Believe me and you shall live with me in eternity."

## 2.Via Quaestio: The Path of Radical Inquiry

Say what you will about PKD, the man was smart. Although self-learned, his voluminous knowledge of religion and philosophy informed everything he did throughout his life. Since Living Information is salvific within the context of Valism, it makes sense that the exercise of the intellect-- rhetoric, dialectic, reason-- allows that Living Information to expand and dwell within the consciousness.

There is a mystical component to Valism, but that mystical component seems to depend upon Grace. You can't "summon" VALIS, or pray to Zebra, or take pills that produce the pink beam. As PKD says in "The Ten Major Principles of the Gnostic Revelation," "You can pass from the delusional prison world into the peaceful kingdom if the True Good God places you under His grace and allows you to see reality through His eyes."[25] However, if you do have a mystical experience, the search for a context in which

---

[25] *ibid.*

to place it becomes just as valuable as the experience itself.

As PKD says in the TCS, "Since the universe is actually composed of information, then it can be said that information will save us. This is the saving gnosis which the Gnostics sought. There is no other road to salvation. However, this information—or more precisely the ability to read and understand this information, the universe as information—can only be made available to us by the Holy Spirit. We cannot find it on our own. Thus it is said that we are saved by the grace of God and not by good works, that all salvation belongs to Christ, who, I say, is a physician." In Valism, gnosis is not a mystical experience. The mystical experience can be a vehicle for gnosis, but gnosis does not equal enlightenment. Gnosis is the secret knowledge of our current state, and the information we receive and process that allows us to place that knowledge in context. This is the essence of the *Via Quaestio*: constant inquiry is necessary to keep one alive and relatively sane (relatively!) within our broken timeline.

## 3. Personal Expression

PKD's attempts at understanding the nature of reality weren't limited to his philosophical ruminations. Indeed, the themes we've been discussing in this essay can be found in his fiction since the very beginning. PKD interacted with the Living Information he'd been granted through his writing; this is an important aspect of Valism that shouldn't be overlooked.

Philip K. Dick was an artist. He was also an aesthete, always sensitive to the beauty contained in his favorite music and poetry. Indeed, music, as a theme, often represents the inbreaking of the Living Information in Dick's work. According to one of the plot summaries of "The Owl in Daylight," the novel he was writing at his time of death, the work would have had a musical composer as its protagonist, and would have discussed, in depth, art as an aspect of divinity.

It is our contention that Valism provides an example of someone possessed by the spirit of art. Whether one is a writer, a painter, a musician, a sculptor, etc., it is more than possible for the divine to express itself through artistic expression than through any other kind of practice. This is one of the reasons PKD's work is so resonant and relevant in the modern world; in a society devoid of Sacred Art, PKD created his own. As such, one of the best ways to practice Valism is to find a way to express one's artistic impulses.

Again, it isn't our intent here to write a book on Valism; rather, it is to initiate a discussion on how we can react to, and interact with, a religious exploration of the work of PKD. The fact is, for a certain subset of people (maybe you, maybe not), PKD's experiences speak to the current state of things. We are trapped; things are not what they seem; more kindness is necessary if we wish to remain human; there is a loving God that wishes to make things better for us.

Philip K. Dick's philosophies aren't generally new ideas. It's not as though "hey, what if the world is, like, an illusion, man?" hasn't been asked since the advent of our ability to differentiate simulacra from simulacrum. However, it is the opinion of the author that the language used by PKD may provide some people with just the right kind of semiotic set to make a little sense of things in this world in which, as PKD says, "No single thing abides; and all things are fucked up."[26]

---

[26] Dick, Philip K. *The Transmigration of Timothy Archer.* Vintage Books 1991.

# Afterword: Thinking!

Here's the thing: If you're crazy enough to go around pursuing the Gnostic Way, you're going to come across a lot of people who tell you that gnosis isn't about "thinking," or that "feeling" or "intuition" are more important than reason and intellect. I should know; I used to be one of those people.

However, once you start really getting into this worldview, you begin to discover that the idea that "thinking" is inferior to "feeling," that intuition trumps reason, is hollow and pointless. And, what's more, it's completely antithetical to the context given by the original Gnostics.

Reason is awesome. The original Gnostics knew it, and made it the cornerstone of their philosophy. Even though a lot of people in alternative spirituality give the intellect a back seat to mystical ambiguity, I believe that it's time to abandon this anti-intellectual approach in favor of a more nuanced spiritual methodology, and the Gnostic Way is a good way to do so.

Another one of the tropes you encounter pretty frequently in this field is that *gnosis* is somehow better than *episteme*—that gnosis is "direct acquaintance," but episteme is just "book learnin'," so it's no good. But that's silly. Heck, it's useful to remember that in the Greek, the terms are often used interchangeably.

Instead, a good friend of mine who has devoted more time and energy to understanding gnosis than anyone I know suggests we try thinking of episteme as cursory knowledge and gnosis as advanced knowledge. He suggests we think of it in terms of mathematics.

Episteme, says my wise friend, is like knowing the quadratic equation, and how to use it. If you have episteme of the quadratic equation, you know that for $ax^2 + bx + c = 0$, the value of x is given by $\dfrac{-b \pm \sqrt{b^2 - 4ac}}{2a}$. You've memorized it, and know when to use it.

**If, however, you have *gnosis* of this equation, you know *why it works*.**

See the difference?

In neither case is "intuition" or "feeling" part of the deal. It's all well and good to claim that gnosis is some kind of fluffy bunny feeling or some kind of 'knowledge of the heart' or some kind of 'experiential knowledge' that exists beyond reason. This simply isn't true.

Gnosis: it *is* what you "think." And, if you've read this text and taken it into serious consideration, so much so that you *understand* it, and you've managed to incorporate the Gnostic Way into your own worldview, congratulations: *you've got gnosis!* Don't let anybody else tell you different.

# OTHER TITLES BY JEREMY PUMA

**This Way: Gnosis Without "Gnosticism"** presents an applied spirituality based on the writings found in the Nag Hammadi Library and Zen Buddhism, for people interested in a simple, mature approach to gnosis that doesn't rely on unprovable claims of apostolic succession or New Age neo-Templar silliness, but instead acknowledges the limitations of the material. If you are looking for a context for a modern approach to gnosis that can be practiced by anyone, alone or within an extant organization 'This Way: Gnosis Without "Gnosticism"' is the book for you.

ISBN/EAN13: 1456539418 / 9781456539412 | Page Count: 120
Also available on Amazon Kindle

**A Gnostic Prayerbook.** These prayers, rites, rituals and devotions are for the independent Gnostic practitioner. Herein, one will find prayers of blessing, consecration, thanksgiving, healing and more, as well as a complete collection of sacramental rites for individual practice. Sacraments contain appropriate rubrics, and rites and rituals presented include the Eucharist, Initiations, Baptism and the mysterious and powerful Mystery of the Five Seals.

ISBN/EAN13: 1470025167 / 9781470025168 | Page Count: 160
Also available on Amazon Kindle